# Singapore

LEVEL **3B**

# MATH

Appropriate for Students in GRADE **4**

# PRACTICE

**Frank Schaffer**
An imprint of Carson-Dellosa Publishing LLC
Greensboro, North Carolina

This book has been correlated to state, common core state, national, and Canadian provincial standards. Visit www.carsondellosa.com to search for and view its correlations to your standards.

Copyright © 2009 Singapore Asian Publications (S) Pte. Ltd.

Frank Schaffer
An imprint of Carson-Dellosa Publishing LLC
PO Box 35665
Greensboro, NC 27425 USA

ISBN 978-0-7682-4003-0
06-193137784

# INTRODUCTION TO SINGAPORE MATH

At an elementary level, some simple mathematical skills can help students understand mathematical principles. These skills are the counting-on, counting-back, and crossing-out methods. Note that these methods are most useful when the numbers are small.

## 1. The Counting-On Method

Used for addition of two numbers. Count on in 1s with the help of a picture or number line.

$$7 + 4 = \mathbf{11}$$

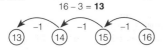

## 2. The Counting-Back Method

Used for subtraction of two numbers. Count back in 1s with the help of a picture or number line.

$$16 - 3 = \mathbf{13}$$

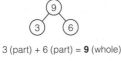

## 3. The Crossing-Out Method

Used for subtraction of two numbers. Cross out the number of items to be taken away. Count the remaining ones to find the answer.

$$20 - 12 = \mathbf{8}$$

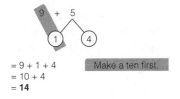

A **number bond** shows the relationship in a simple addition or subtraction problem. The number bond is based on the concept "part-part-whole." This concept is useful in teaching simple addition and subtraction to young children.

To find a whole, students must add the two parts.
To find a part, students must subtract the other part from the whole.

The different types of number bonds are illustrated below.

## 1. Number Bond (single digits)

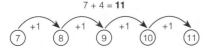

$$3 \text{ (part)} + 6 \text{ (part)} = \mathbf{9} \text{ (whole)}$$
$$9 \text{ (whole)} - 3 \text{ (part)} = \mathbf{6} \text{ (part)}$$
$$9 \text{ (whole)} - 6 \text{ (part)} = \mathbf{3} \text{ (part)}$$

## 2. Addition Number Bond (single digits)

= 9 + 1 + 4        Make a ten first.
= 10 + 4
= **14**

## 3. Addition Number Bond (double and single digits)

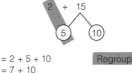

= 2 + 5 + 10        Regroup 15 into 5 and 10.
= 7 + 10
= **17**

## 4. Subtraction Number Bond (double and single digits)

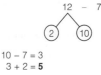

$$10 - 7 = 3$$
$$3 + 2 = \mathbf{5}$$

## 5. Subtraction Number Bond (double digits)

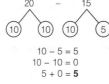

$$10 - 5 = 5$$
$$10 - 10 = 0$$
$$5 + 0 = \mathbf{5}$$

Students should understand that multiplication is repeated addition and that division is the grouping of all items into equal sets.

## 1. Repeated Addition (Multiplication)

Mackenzie eats 2 rolls a day. How many rolls does she eat in 5 days?

$$2 + 2 + 2 + 2 + 2 = 10$$
$$5 \times 2 = 10$$

She eats **10** rolls in 5 days.

## 2. The Grouping Method (Division)

Mrs. Lee makes 14 sandwiches. She gives all the sandwiches equally to 7 friends. How many sandwiches does each friend receive?

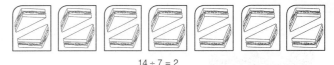

$$14 \div 7 = 2$$

Each friend receives **2** sandwiches.

One of the basic but essential math skills students should acquire is to perform the 4 operations of whole numbers and fractions. Each of these methods is illustrated below.

## 1. The Adding-Without-Regrouping Method

```
  H T O
  3 2 1        O: Ones
+ 5 6 8        T: Tens
---------
  8 8 9        H: Hundreds
```

Since no regrouping is required, add the digits in each place value accordingly.

## 2. The Adding-by-Regrouping Method

```
  H T O
  ¹4 9 2       O: Ones
+ 1 5 3        T: Tens
---------
  6 4 5        H: Hundreds
```

In this example, regroup 14 tens into 1 hundred 4 tens.

Singapore Math Practice Level 3B

### 3. The Adding-by-Regrouping-Twice Method

$$
\begin{array}{ccc}
H & T & O \\
{}^{1}2 & {}^{1}8 & 6 \\
+\ 3 & 6 & 5 \\
\hline
6 & 5 & 1
\end{array}
$$

O: Ones
T: Tens
H: Hundreds

Regroup twice in this example.
First, regroup 11 ones into 1 ten 1 one.
Second, regroup 15 tens into 1 hundred 5 tens.

### 4. The Subtracting-Without-Regrouping Method

$$
\begin{array}{ccc}
H & T & O \\
7 & 3 & 9 \\
-\ 3 & 2 & 5 \\
\hline
4 & 1 & 4
\end{array}
$$

O: Ones
T: Tens
H: Hundreds

Since no regrouping is required, subtract the digits in each place value accordingly.

### 5. The Subtracting-by-Regrouping Method

$$
\begin{array}{ccc}
H & T & O \\
5 & {}^{7}8 & {}^{11}1 \\
-\ 2 & 4 & 7 \\
\hline
3 & 3 & 4
\end{array}
$$

O: Ones
T: Tens
H: Hundreds

In this example, students cannot subtract 7 ones from 1 one. So, regroup the tens and ones. Regroup 8 tens 1 one into 7 tens 11 ones.

### 6. The Subtracting-by-Regrouping-Twice Method

$$
\begin{array}{ccc}
H & T & O \\
{}^{7}8 & {}^{9}0 & {}^{10}0 \\
-\ 5 & 9 & 3 \\
\hline
2 & 0 & 7
\end{array}
$$

O: Ones
T: Tens
H: Hundreds

In this example, students cannot subtract 3 ones from 0 ones and 9 tens from 0 tens. So, regroup the hundreds, tens, and ones. Regroup 8 hundreds into 7 hundreds 9 tens 10 ones.

### 7. The Multiplying-Without-Regrouping Method

$$
\begin{array}{cc}
T & O \\
2 & 4 \\
\times & 2 \\
\hline
4 & 8
\end{array}
$$

O: Ones
T: Tens

Since no regrouping is required, multiply the digit in each place value by the multiplier accordingly.

### 8. The Multiplying-With-Regrouping Method

$$
\begin{array}{ccc}
H & T & O \\
{}^{1}3 & {}^{2}4 & 9 \\
\times & & 3 \\
\hline
1,0 & 4 & 7
\end{array}
$$

O: Ones
T: Tens
H: Hundreds

In this example, regroup 27 ones into 2 tens 7 ones, and 14 tens into 1 hundred 4 tens.

### 9. The Dividing-Without-Regrouping Method

$$
\begin{array}{r}
241 \\
2\overline{)482} \\
-4 \phantom{00} \\
\hline
8 \phantom{0} \\
-8 \phantom{0} \\
\hline
2 \\
-2 \\
\hline
0
\end{array}
$$

Since no regrouping is required, divide the digit in each place value by the divisor accordingly.

### 10. The Dividing-With-Regrouping Method

$$
\begin{array}{r}
166 \\
5\overline{)830} \\
-5 \phantom{00} \\
\hline
33 \phantom{0} \\
-30 \phantom{0} \\
\hline
30 \\
-30 \\
\hline
0
\end{array}
$$

In this example, regroup 3 hundreds into 30 tens and add 3 tens to make 33 tens. Regroup 3 tens into 30 ones.

### 11. The Addition-of-Fractions Method

$$
\frac{1}{6} \times \frac{2}{2} + \frac{1}{4} \times \frac{3}{3} = \frac{2}{12} + \frac{3}{12} = \frac{5}{12}
$$

Always remember to make the denominators common before adding the fractions.

### 12. The Subtraction-of-Fractions Method

$$
\frac{1}{2} \times \frac{5}{5} - \frac{1}{5} \times \frac{2}{2} = \frac{5}{10} - \frac{2}{10} = \frac{3}{10}
$$

Always remembers to make the denominators common before subtracting the fractions.

### 13. The Multiplication-of-Fractions Method

$$
\frac{{}^{1}3}{5} \times \frac{1}{{}_{3}9} = \frac{1}{15}
$$

When the numerator and the denominator have a common multiple, reduce them to their lowest fractions.

### 14. The Division-of-Fractions Method

$$
\frac{7}{9} \div \frac{1}{6} = \frac{7}{{}_{3}9} \times \frac{{}^{2}6}{1} = \frac{14}{3} = 4\frac{2}{3}
$$

When dividing fractions, first change the division sign ($\div$) to the multiplication sign ($\times$). Then, switch the numerator and denominator of the fraction on the right hand side. Multiply the fractions in the usual way.

**Model drawing** is an effective strategy used to solve math word problems. It is a visual representation of the information in word problems using bar units. By drawing the models, students will know of the variables given in the problem, the variables to find, and even the methods used to solve the problem.

Drawing models is also a versatile strategy. It can be applied to simple word problems involving addition, subtraction, multiplication, and division. It can also be applied to word problems related to fractions, decimals, percentage, and ratio.

The use of models also trains students to think in an algebraic manner, which uses symbols for representation.

The different types of bar models used to solve word problems are illustrated below.

### 1. The model that involves addition

Melissa has 50 blue beads and 20 red beads. How many beads does she have altogether?

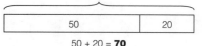

$$50 + 20 = \mathbf{70}$$

### 2. The model that involves subtraction

Ben and Andy have 90 toy cars. Andy has 60 toy cars. How many toy cars does Ben have?

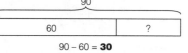

$$90 - 60 = \mathbf{30}$$

### 3. The model that involves comparison

Mr. Simons has 150 magazines and 110 books in his study. How many more magazines than books does he have?

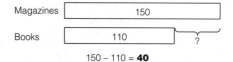

$$150 - 110 = \mathbf{40}$$

### 4. The model that involves two items with a difference

A pair of shoes costs $109. A leather bag costs $241 more than the pair of shoes. How much is the leather bag?

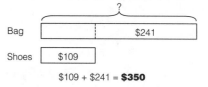

$$\$109 + \$241 = \mathbf{\$350}$$

Singapore Math Practice Level 3B

## 5. The model that involves multiples

Mrs. Drew buys 12 apples. She buys 3 times as many oranges as apples. She also buys 3 times as many cherries as oranges. How many pieces of fruit does she buy altogether?

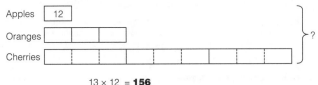

$13 \times 12 = \textbf{156}$

## 6. The model that involves multiples and difference

There are 15 students in Class A. There are 5 more students in Class B than in Class A. There are 3 times as many students in Class C than in Class A. How many students are there altogether in the three classes?

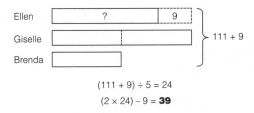

$(5 \times 15) + 5 = \textbf{80}$

## 7. The model that involves creating a whole

Ellen, Giselle, and Brenda bake 111 muffins. Giselle bakes twice as many muffins as Brenda. Ellen bakes 9 fewer muffins than Giselle. How many muffins does Ellen bake?

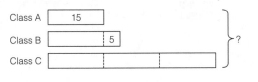

$(111 + 9) \div 5 = 24$

$(2 \times 24) - 9 = \textbf{39}$

## 8. The model that involves sharing

There are 183 tennis balls in Basket A and 97 tennis balls in Basket B. How many tennis balls must be transferred from Basket A to Basket B so that both baskets contain the same number of tennis balls?

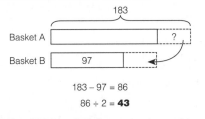

$183 - 97 = 86$

$86 \div 2 = \textbf{43}$

## 9. The model that involves fractions

George had 355 marbles. He lost $\frac{1}{5}$ of the marbles and gave $\frac{1}{4}$ of the remaining marbles to his brother. How many marbles did he have left?

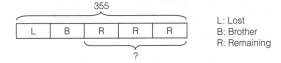

L: Lost
B: Brother
R: Remaining

5 parts → 355 marbles

1 part → 355 ÷ 5 = 71 marbles

3 parts → 3 × 71 = **213** marbles

## 10. The model that involves ratio

Aaron buys a tie and a belt. The prices of the tie and belt are in the ratio 2 : 5. If both items cost $539,

(a) what is the price of the tie?

(b) what is the price of the belt?

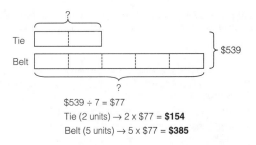

$\$539 \div 7 = \$77$

Tie (2 units) → 2 × $77 = **$154**

Belt (5 units) → 5 × $77 = **$385**

## 11. The model that involves comparison of fractions

Jack's height is $\frac{2}{3}$ of Leslie's height. Leslie's height is $\frac{3}{4}$ of Lindsay's height. If Lindsay is 160 cm tall, find Jack's height and Leslie's height.

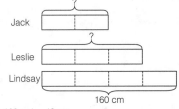

1 unit → 160 ÷ 4 = 40 cm

Leslie's height (3 units) → 3 × 40 = **120 cm**

Jack's height (2 units) → 2 × 40 = **80 cm**

Thinking skills and strategies are important in mathematical problem solving. These skills are applied when students think through the math problems to solve them. Below are some commonly used thinking skills and strategies applied in mathematical problem solving.

### 1. Comparing

*Comparing* is a form of thinking skill that students can apply to identify similarities and differences.

When comparing numbers, look carefully at each digit before deciding if a number is greater or less than the other. Students might also use a number line for comparison when there are more numbers.

Example:

**3 is greater than 2 but smaller than 7.**

### 2. Sequencing

A sequence shows the order of a series of numbers. *Sequencing* is a form of thinking skill that requires students to place numbers in a particular order. There are many terms in a sequence. The terms refer to the numbers in a sequence.

To place numbers in a correct order, students must first find a rule that generates the sequence. In a simple math sequence, students can either add or subtract to find the unknown terms in the sequence.

Example: Find the 7th term in the sequence below.

| 1,<br>1st<br>term | 4,<br>2nd<br>term | 7,<br>3rd<br>term | 10,<br>4th<br>term | 13,<br>5th<br>term | 16<br>6th<br>term | ?<br>7th<br>term |
|---|---|---|---|---|---|---|

Step 1:   This sequence is in an increasing order.

Step 2:   $4 - 1 = 3$          $7 - 4 = 3$
          The difference between two consecutive terms is 3.

Step 3:   $16 + 3 = 19$
          The 7th term is **19**.

### 3. Visualization

*Visualization* is a problem solving strategy that can help students visualize a problem through the use of physical objects. Students will play a more active role in solving the problem by manipulating these objects.

The main advantage of using this strategy is the mobility of information in the process of solving the problem. When students make a wrong step in the process, they can retrace the step without erasing or canceling it.

The other advantage is that this strategy helps develop a better understanding of the problem or solution through visual objects or images. In this way, students will be better able to remember how to solve these types of problems.

Some of the commonly used objects for this strategy are toothpicks, straws, cards, strings, water, sand, pencils, paper, and dice.

### 4. Look for a Pattern

This strategy requires the use of observational and analytical skills. Students have to observe the given data to find a pattern in order to solve the problem. Math word problems that involve the use of this strategy usually have repeated numbers or patterns.

Example: Find the sum of all the numbers from 1 to 100.

Step 1: Simplify the problem.
Find the sum of 1, 2, 3, 4, 5, 6, 7, 8, 9, and 10.

Step 2: Look for a pattern.

$1 + 10 = 11$ $\quad\quad$ $2 + 9 = 11$ $\quad\quad$ $3 + 8 = 11$
$4 + 7 = 11$ $\quad\quad$ $5 + 6 = 11$

Step 3: Describe the pattern.
When finding the sum of 1 to 10, add the first and last numbers to get a result of 11. Then, add the second and second last numbers to get the same result. The pattern continues until all the numbers from 1 to 10 are added. There will be 5 pairs of such results. Since each addition equals 11, the answer is then $5 \times 11 = 55$.

Step 4: Use the pattern to find the answer.
Since there are 5 pairs in the sum of 1 to 10, there should be (10 × 5 = 50 pairs) in the sum of 1 to 100.

Note that the addition for each pair is not equal to 11 now. The addition for each pair is now $(1 + 100 = 101)$.
$$50 \times 101 = 5050$$
The sum of all the numbers from 1 to 100 is **5,050**.

### 5. Working Backward

The strategy of working backward applies only to a specific type of math word problem. These word problems state the end result, and students are required to find the total number. In order to solve these word problems, students have to work backward by thinking through the correct sequence of events. The strategy of working backward allows students to use their logical reasoning and sequencing to find the answers.

Example: Sarah has a piece of ribbon. She cuts the ribbon into 4 equal parts. Each part is then cut into 3 smaller equal parts. If the length of each small part is 35 cm, how long is the piece of ribbon?
$$3 \times 35 = 105 \text{ cm}$$
$$4 \times 105 = 420 \text{ cm}$$
The piece of ribbon is **420 cm**.

### 6. The Before-After Concept

The *Before-After* concept lists all the relevant data before and after an event. Students can then compare the differences and eventually solve the problems. Usually, the Before-After concept and the mathematical model go hand in hand to solve math word problems. Note that the Before-After concept can be applied only to a certain type of math word problem, which trains students to think sequentially.

Example: Kelly has 4 times as much money as Joey. After Kelly uses some money to buy a tennis racquet, and Joey uses $30 to buy a pair of pants, Kelly has twice as much money as Joey. If Joey has $98 in the beginning,
(a) how much money does Kelly have in the end?
(b) how much money does Kelly spend on the tennis racquet?

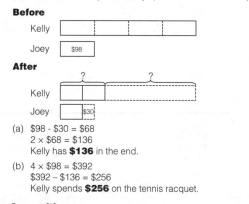

(a) $98 - $30 = $68
$2 \times $68 = $136
Kelly has **$136** in the end.

(b) $4 \times $98 = $392
$392 - $136 = $256
Kelly spends **$256** on the tennis racquet.

### 7. Making Supposition

*Making supposition* is commonly known as "making an assumption." Students can use this strategy to solve certain types of math word problems. Making

assumptions will eliminate some possibilities and simplifies the word problems by providing a boundary of values to work within.

Example: Mrs. Jackson bought 100 pieces of candy for all the students in her class. How many pieces of candy would each student receive if there were 25 students in her class?

In the above word problem, assume that each student received the same number of pieces. This eliminates the possibilities that some students would receive more than others due to good behaviour, better results, or any other reason.

### 8. Representation of Problem

In problem solving, students often use representations in the solutions to show their understanding of the problems. Using representations also allow students to understand the mathematical concepts and relationships as well as to manipulate the information presented in the problems. Examples of representations are diagrams and lists or tables.

Diagrams allow students to consolidate or organize the information given in the problems. By drawing a diagram, students can see the problem clearly and solve it effectively.

A list or table can help students organize information that is useful for analysis. After analyzing, students can then see a pattern, which can be used to solve the problem.

### 9. Guess and Check

One of the most important and effective problem-solving techniques is *Guess and Check*. It is also known as *Trial and Error*. As the name suggests, students have to guess the answer to a problem and check if that guess is correct. If the guess is wrong, students will make another guess. This will continue until the guess is correct.

It is beneficial to keep a record of all the guesses and checks in a table. In addition, a *Comments* column can be included. This will enable students to analyze their guess (if it is too high or too low) and improve on the next guess. Be careful; this problem-solving technique can be tiresome without systematic or logical guesses.

Example: Jessica had 15 coins. Some of them were 10-cent coins and the rest were 5-cent coins. The total amount added up to $1.25. How many coins of each kind were there?

Use the guess-and-check method.

| Number of 10¢ Coins | Value | Number of 5¢ Coins | Value | Total Number of Coins | Total Value |
|---|---|---|---|---|---|
| 7 | $7 \times 10¢ = 70¢$ | 8 | $8 \times 5¢ = 40¢$ | 7 + 8 = 15 | 70¢ + 40¢ = 110¢ = $1.10 |
| 8 | $8 \times 10¢ = 80¢$ | 7 | $7 \times 5¢ = 35¢$ | 8 + 7 = 15 | 80¢ + 35¢ = 115¢ = $1.15 |
| 10 | $10 \times 10¢ = 100¢$ | 5 | $5 \times 5¢ = 25¢$ | 10 + 5 = 15 | 100¢ + 25¢ = 125¢ = $1.25 |

There were **ten** 10-cent coins and **five** 5-cent coins.

### 10. Restate the Problem

When solving challenging math problems, conventional methods may not be workable. Instead, restating the problem will enable students to see some challenging problems in a different light so that they can better understand them.

The strategy of restating the problem is to "say" the problem in a different and clearer way. However, students have to ensure that the main idea of the problem is not altered.

How do students restate a math problem?

First, read and understand the problem. Gather the given facts and unknowns. Note any condition(s) that have to be satisfied.

Next, restate the problem. Imagine narrating this problem to a friend. Present the given facts, unknown(s), and condition(s). Students may want to write the "revised" problem. Once the "revised" problem is analyzed, students should be able to think of an appropriate strategy to solve it.

### 11. Simplify the Problem

One of the commonly used strategies in mathematical problem solving is simplification of the problem. When a problem is simplified, it can be "broken down" into two or more smaller parts. Students can then solve the parts systematically to get to the final answer.

Singapore Math Practice Level 3B

# Table of Contents

Introduction to Singapore Math.................................................3

Learning Outcomes...........................................................9

Formula Sheet .............................................................10

Unit 10:   Money ..........................................................13

Unit 11:   Length, Mass, and Volume .........................................23

Unit 12:   Problem Solving (Length, Mass, and Volume).........................31

Review 1   ................................................................38

Unit 13:   Bar Graphs......................................................43

Unit 14:   Fractions.......................................................52

Unit 15:   Time...........................................................61

Review 2   ................................................................70

Unit 16:   Angles..........................................................75

Unit 17:   Perpendicular and Parallel Lines...................................84

Unit 18:   Area and Perimeter ..............................................93

Review 3   ...............................................................101

Final Review ............................................................108

Challenge Questions .....................................................115

Solutions .............................................................117

# LEARNING OUTCOMES

## Unit 10  Money
Students should be able to
- add and subtract money in dollars and cents.
- solve story problems related to money.

## Unit 11  Length, Mass, and Volume
Students should be able to
- state length in kilometers, meters, or centimeters.
- state mass in kilograms and grams.
- read the correct mass on scales.
- state volume in liters and milliliters.
- read the correct volume in measuring beakers.

## Unit 12  Problem Solving (Length, Mass, and Volume)
Students should be able to
- solve story problems related to length, mass, and volume.

## Review 1
This review tests students' understanding of Units 10, 11, & 12.

## Unit 13  Bar Graphs
Students should be able to
- read and interpret data from bar graphs.
- draw bar graphs based on given data.

## Unit 14  Fractions
Students should be able to
- recognize equivalent fractions.
- list up to the first eight equivalent fractions.
- complete equivalent fractions.
- state a fraction in its simplest form.
- compare and arrange fractions.
- add and subtract fractions.

## Unit 15  Time
Students should be able to
- read and draw the correct time.
- state time in minutes or hours and minutes.
- find the length between two different times.
- find the starting time or ending time.
- add and subtract time in hours and minutes.
- solve story problems related to time.

## Review 2
This review tests students' understanding of Units 13, 14, & 15.

## Unit 16  Angles
Students should be able to
- identify angles and right angles.
- identify angles in 2-dimensional and 3-dimensional objects.
- identify the number of sides and angles in a figure.

## Unit 17  Perpendicular and Parallel Lines
Students should be able to
- identify and draw perpendicular lines.
- identify and draw parallel lines.

## Unit 18  Area and Perimeter
Students should be able to
- find the area of figures in $cm^2$, $m^2$, $in.^2$, or $ft.^2$.
- find the perimeter of figures.
- use the formula to find the area of figures.
- solve story problems related to area and perimeter.

## Review 3
This review tests students' understanding of Units 16, 17, & 18.

## Final Review
This review is an excellent assessment of students' understanding of all the topics in this book.

# FORMULA SHEET

## Unit 10  Money

### Adding Money

There are three ways to add money.

❶ Add the dollars first.
Add the cents next.
Add the cents to the dollars.

Example: What is $10.20 + $28.35?

$10 + $28 = $38
20¢ + 35¢ = 55¢
$38 + 55¢ = **$38.55**

❷ Round up one of the addends (A) to the nearest dollar.
Add the other addend (B) and the round addend.
Subtract the difference between the round addend and addend (A) from the sum.

Example: What is $32.50 + $0.90?

$32.50 + $1 = $33.50
$33.50 – 10¢ = **$33.40**

❸ Add by formal algorithm.

Example: What is $61.80 + $12.70?

$$\begin{array}{r} \$6\overset{1}{1}.80 \\ +\$12.70 \\ \hline \mathbf{\$74.50} \end{array}$$

Make sure the dollar sign ($) and decimal point (.) align. If one of the addends does not have cents, add two zeros after the decimal point.

### Subtracting Money

There are three ways to subtract money.

❶ Subtract the dollars first.
Subtract the cents next.
Add the cents to the dollars.

Example: What is $50.90 – $12.60?

$50 – $12 = $38
90¢ – 60¢ = 30¢
$38 + 30¢ = **$38.30**

❷ Round the second term (A) to the nearest dollar. Subtract the rounded term from the first term (B). Add the difference between the rounded amount and the original amount to the result.

Example: What is $49.60 – $8.70?

B      A
$49.60 – $9 = $40.60
$40.60 + 30¢ = **$40.90**

❸ Add by formal algorithm.

Example: What is $88.00 – $54.60?

$$\begin{array}{r} \$8\overset{7}{8}.\overset{10}{0}0 \\ -\$54.60 \\ \hline \mathbf{\$33.40} \end{array}$$

Make sure the dollar sign ($) and decimal point (.) align. If one of the amounts does not have cents, add two zeros after the decimal point.

## Unit 11    Length, Mass, and Volume

### Length

Units of measurement: kilometers (km), meters (m), and centimeters (cm)

1 km = 1,000 m
1 m = 100 cm

### Mass

Units of measurement: kilograms (kg) and grams (g)

1 kg = 1,000 g

When reading a scale,
• find how many grams or kilograms each small marking stands for,
• note the marking that the needle points to.

The marking pointed to by the needle shows the mass of an item.

### Volume

Units of measurement: liters (L) and milliliters (mL)

1 L = 1,000 mL

**Capacity** is the total amount of liquid that a container can hold.
**Volume** is the amount of liquid in a container.

When reading the scale on a measuring container,
• find how many liters or milliliters each small marking stands for,
• note the liquid level that coincides with the marking on the measuring container.

The marking that coincides with the liquid level shows the capacity or volume of liquid in the measuring container.

## Unit 12    Problem Solving (Length, Mass, and Volume)

Below is a suggested procedure when solving story problems.
1. Read the story problem carefully.
2. Find what you are supposed to solve in the story problem.
3. Draw model(s) for better understanding.
4. Write a number sentence. You have to write two number sentences when working on a two-step story problem.
5. Write the formal algorithm on the right side of the space.
6. Write a statement to answer the question in the story problem. You can underline the final answer in the statement.

## Unit 13 Bar Graphs

A bar graph is a single chart that displays bars representing certain values along its axis.

Bar graphs organize data effectively. This helps in easy comparison and problem solving.

When interpreting data from bar graphs, note the scale of the axis.

Two types of bar graphs are introduced in this book. They are vertical and horizontal bar graphs.

An example of a vertical bar graph is shown below.

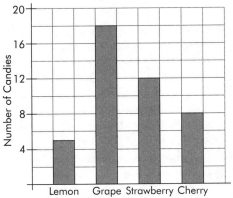

**Flavors of Candy**

An example of a horizontal bar graph is shown below.

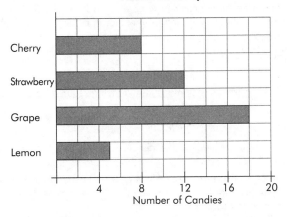

**Flavors of Candy**

## Unit 14 Fractions

**Equivalent fractions** are fractions that have the same value.

Examples: $\frac{1}{3}$, $\frac{2}{6}$, $\frac{3}{9}$, and $\frac{4}{12}$

In order to find an equivalent fraction, multiply both the numerator and denominator of a fraction by the same number.

Example: $\frac{3 \times 2}{5 \times 2} = \frac{6}{10}$

### Comparing fractions

• When fractions have the same denominator, just compare their numerators.

The greater the numerator, the greater the fraction.
• When fractions have the same numerator, just compare their denominators.
The greater the denominator, the smaller the fraction.
• When fractions do not have the same denominator, make these fractions equivalent first.
It is easier to compare when the fractions have the same denominator.

### Adding fractions

1. Make sure all addends have the same denominator.
   If they do not, find the equivalent fractions.
2. Add all numerators of each fraction to get the result.
3. Write the final fraction in its simplest form if required.

### Subtracting fractions

1. Make sure all terms have the same denominator.
   If they do not, find the equivalent fractions.

   A whole (1) can be expressed in equivalent fractions like $\frac{2}{2}$, $\frac{3}{3}$, $\frac{4}{4}$, $\frac{5}{5}$, $\frac{6}{6}$, $\frac{7}{7}$, $\frac{8}{8}$, $\frac{9}{9}$, $\frac{10}{10}$, $\frac{11}{11}$, and $\frac{12}{12}$.
2. Subtract all numerators of each fraction to get the result.
3. Write the final fraction in its simplest form if required.

## Unit 15 Time

### Telling time

When the minute hand points before/to 6 on the face of a clock, use the word *after*.

When using the word *after*, count the minutes that are past a certain hour.

Example:

10:20 is **20 minutes after 10**.

When the minute hand has moved past 6 on the face of a clock, use the word *to*.

When using the word *to*, count the minutes needed to move to the next hour.

Example:

12:45 is **15 minutes to 1**.

### Converting hours and minutes

1 hour = 60 minutes
• When converting hours to minutes, multiply the number of hours by 60.
  Example: 7 hr. = 7 × 60 min. = 420 min.
• When converting minutes to hours, divide the number of hours by 60.
  Example: 540 min. = 540 min. ÷ 60 min. = 9 hr.

### Adding time

1. Add the minutes. If the total is more than 60, regroup the hours and minutes.
2. Add the hours. Remember to add an hour from the regrouping if necessary.

Singapore Math Practice Level 3B

<u>Subtracting time</u>
1. Subtract the minutes. If this is not possible, regroup the hours and minutes.
2. Subtract the hours.

<u>Finding the length of time</u>
A timeline is used to find the length of time in minutes and hours. It can also be used to find the time before/after a certain time.

Example:

There are **2 hr. 20 min.** from 4:30 P.M. to 6:50 P.M.
2 hr. 20 min. before 6:50 P.M. is **4:30 P.M.**
2 hr. 20 min. after 4:30 P.M. is **6:50 P.M.**

## Unit 16   Angles
When two straight lines meet, an angle is formed.

Example:

A right angle is formed when a vertical line meets a horizontal line.

Symbol: ⌐

Example:

right angle

The size of the angle is measured in degrees. A right angle measures 90 degrees.

Angles can be found in 2-dimensional shapes and 3-dimensional objects.
The number of sides of a 2-dimensional shape and the number of angles in that shape are usually the same.

Example:

This 2-dimensional shape has 4 sides and 4 angles.

## Unit 17   Perpendicular and Parallel Lines
When two straight lines meet and form a right angle, these two lines are known as **perpendicular lines**.

Symbol: ⊥

Examples:

When drawing perpendicular lines,
1. draw two straight lines with a ruler,
2. make sure a right angle is formed when these two lines meet.

When two straight lines are equal distance away from each other and do not meet, they are known as **parallel lines**.

Symbol: //

Examples:

When drawing parallel lines,
1. draw two straight lines with a ruler,
2. make sure one line is equal distance away from the other line at all points.

## Unit 18   Area and Perimeter
<u>Area</u>
Area is defined as the size of a surface.
Units of measurement: square centimeters (cm²), square meters (m²), square inches (in.²), and square feet (ft.²).

<u>Finding area of a figure in a grid of 1-cm and 1-in. squares</u>
Count the number of squares that make up the figure.

<u>Finding area of a rectangle</u>
Area = Length × Width
Make sure the units of measurement for both length and width are the same.

<u>Finding area of a square</u>
Area = Length × Length
Make sure the units of measurement for all four sides are the same.

<u>Perimeter</u>
Perimeter is defined as the distance around a figure or an object.
Units of measurement: centimeters (cm), meters (m), inches (in.), and feet (ft.)

<u>Finding perimeter of a figure in a grid of 1-cm and 1-in. squares</u>
Count the number of lines that make up the figure.

<u>Finding perimeter of a rectangle</u>
Add the length of its four sides.

<u>Finding perimeter of a square</u>
Add the length of its four sides.
Alternatively, multiply the length of one side by 4 as all sides of a square are equal.

# Unit 10: MONEY

**Examples:**

1. What is $27.35 + $12.35?

   $27 + $12 = $39

   35¢ + 35¢ = 70¢

   $39 + 70¢ = **$39.70**

2. What is $98.50 – $14.90?

   $98.50 – $15.00 = $83.50

   $83.50 + 10¢ = **$83.60**

3. Jessie starts with $25. She spends $6.90 on a notebook and $2.80 on a pen. How much money does Jessie have left?

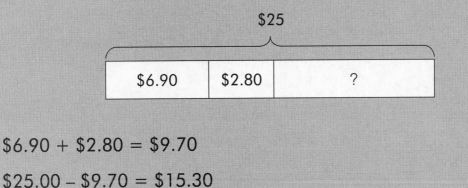

$25

| $6.90 | $2.80 | ? |

   $6.90 + $2.80 = $9.70

   $25.00 – $9.70 = $15.30

Jessie has **$15.30** left.

Singapore Math Practice Level 3B

# Write the correct answers on the lines.

1.  $5.35 + $3.00 = $_____

2.  $43.20 + $8.00 = $_____

3.  $14.00 + $90.75 = $_____

4.  $30.00 + $68.90 = $_____

5.  $9.05 + $0.55 = $_____

6.  $24.00 + $0.90 = $_____

7.  $0.80 + $70.00 = $_____

8.  $82.40 + $6.80 = $_____

9.  $53.60 + $2.25 = $_____

10. $43.50 + $1.80 = $_____

# Fill in each blank with the correct answer.

> *Example:*
> $$\$25.40 + \$0.90 = \$25.40 + \$1.00$$
> $$= \$26.40 - 10¢$$
> $$= \underline{\$26.30}$$

11. $18.20 + $0.70 = $_____ + $_____

             = $_____ – _____¢

             = $_____

Singapore Math Practice Level 3B

12. $26.90 + $0.80 = $_____ + $_____

              = $_____ – _____¢

              = $_____

13. $72.50 + $0.90 = $_____ + $_____

              = $_____ – _____¢

              = $_____

14. $59.60 + $0.80 = $_____ + $_____

              = $_____ – _____¢

              = $_____

15. $76.40 + $0.70 = $_____ + $_____

              = $_____ – _____¢

              = $_____

## Solve the addition problems below. Show your work.

16.     $ 2 3 . 5 0
       + $ 1 3 . 2 0
       ——————

18.     $ 5 1 5 . 5 5
      + $   7 9 . 2 5
      ——————

17.     $ 8 6 . 7 5
       + $ 3 7 . 4 5
       ——————

19.     $ 4 . 3 5
     +  $ 0 . 9 0
     ——————

20.     $ 7 3 . 2 0
     + $ 1 8 . 0 0
    —————————

23.     $ 5 6 . 2 0
     + $ 6 4 . 1 5
    —————————

21.     $ 1 2 5 . 8 0
     + $ 2 1 4 . 4 0
    —————————

24.     $ 4 9 . 7 0
     + $ 2 8 . 5 0
    —————————

22.     $ 2 1 7 . 0 0
     + $ 1 4 2 . 8 5
    —————————

25.     $ 6 7 . 9 0
     + $ 1 7 . 7 0
    —————————

## Write the correct answers on the lines.

26. $39.40 – $5.00 = $_____

27. $78.55 – $4.00 = $_____

28. $36.70 – $0.60 = $_____

29. $82.75 – $0.20 = $_____

30. $48.60 – $0.45 = $_____

31. $99.50 – $0.35 = $_____

32. $87.30 – $4.10 = $_____

33. $69.55 – $3.35 = $_____

34. $92.60 – $1.30 = $_____

35. $58.80 – $7.50 = $_____

16

**Fill in each blank with the correct answer.**

> *Example:*
> $$\$80.50 - \$0.90 = \$80.50 - \$1.00$$
> $$= \$79.50 + 10¢$$
> $$= \underline{\$79.60}$$

36.  $\$67.40 - \$0.80 = \$\underline{\hspace{1.5cm}} - \$\underline{\hspace{1.5cm}}$

$$= \$\underline{\hspace{1.5cm}} + \underline{\hspace{1.5cm}}¢$$

$$= \$\underline{\hspace{1.5cm}}$$

37.  $\$46.20 - \$0.70 = \$\underline{\hspace{1.5cm}} - \$\underline{\hspace{1.5cm}}$

$$= \$\underline{\hspace{1.5cm}} + \underline{\hspace{1.5cm}}¢$$

$$= \$\underline{\hspace{1.5cm}}$$

38.  $\$28.30 - \$0.90 = \$\underline{\hspace{1.5cm}} - \$\underline{\hspace{1.5cm}}$

$$= \$\underline{\hspace{1.5cm}} + \underline{\hspace{1.5cm}}¢$$

$$= \$\underline{\hspace{1.5cm}}$$

39.  $\$70.60 - \$0.80 = \$\underline{\hspace{1.5cm}} - \$\underline{\hspace{1.5cm}}$

$$= \$\underline{\hspace{1.5cm}} + \underline{\hspace{1.5cm}}¢$$

$$= \$\underline{\hspace{1.5cm}}$$

40.  $\$45.20 - \$0.90 = \$\underline{\hspace{1.5cm}} - \$\underline{\hspace{1.5cm}}$

$$= \$\underline{\hspace{1.5cm}} + \underline{\hspace{1.5cm}}¢$$

$$= \$\underline{\hspace{1.5cm}}$$

Singapore Math Practice Level 3B

**Solve the subtraction problems below. Show your work.**

41.
$$
\begin{array}{r}
\$\ 7.80 \\
-\$\ 3.50 \\
\hline
\end{array}
$$

46.
$$
\begin{array}{r}
\$\ 143.05 \\
-\$\ \ \ 21.80 \\
\hline
\end{array}
$$

42.
$$
\begin{array}{r}
\$\ 50.00 \\
-\$\ \ 5.60 \\
\hline
\end{array}
$$

47.
$$
\begin{array}{r}
\$\ 955.60 \\
-\$\ \ \ 89.45 \\
\hline
\end{array}
$$

43.
$$
\begin{array}{r}
\$\ 280.50 \\
-\$\ \ \ 66.60 \\
\hline
\end{array}
$$

48.
$$
\begin{array}{r}
\$\ 49.25 \\
-\$\ \ 5.60 \\
\hline
\end{array}
$$

44.
$$
\begin{array}{r}
\$\ 23.10 \\
-\$\ \ 2.30 \\
\hline
\end{array}
$$

49.
$$
\begin{array}{r}
\$\ 10.00 \\
-\$\ \ 3.45 \\
\hline
\end{array}
$$

45.
$$
\begin{array}{r}
\$\ 758.70 \\
-\$\ 329.40 \\
\hline
\end{array}
$$

50.
$$
\begin{array}{r}
\$\ 659.20 \\
-\$\ \ 92.25 \\
\hline
\end{array}
$$

Singapore Math Practice Level 3B

51. Below are some items sold in a store.

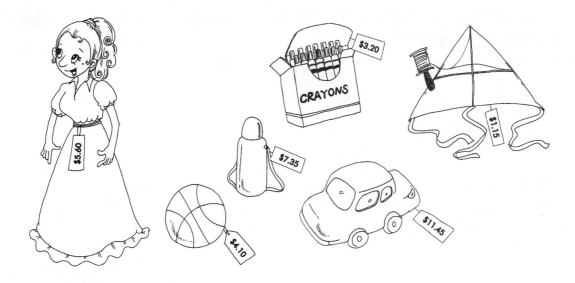

(a) Janice bought a box of crayons and a doll. How much did she pay altogether?

$_____

(b) Maggie bought a doll and a water bottle. How much did she pay for the items?

$_____

(c) Paul had only $5. List the two things that Paul could buy with that amount of money.

_____

(d) Mike bought a toy car and a kite. He gave the cashier $20. How much change would he receive?

$_____

(e) How much more did the water bottle cost than the ball?

$_____

Singapore Math Practice Level 3B

**Solve the following story problems. Show your work in the space below.**

52. Ashley buys a can of orange juice for $1.10 and a box of cereal for $3.50. How much does Ashley pay altogether?

53. Karly bought a pair of shoes and two blouses for $75.35. If she gave the cashier $100, how much change would she receive?

54. Desmond gave $500 to his parents. His brother gave them $200 more than Desmond. How much did his parents receive altogether?

Singapore Math Practice Level 3B

55. Carmen spends $75.70 on her phone bill, $125 on her car, and $360 on food each month. How much does she spend altogether each month?

56. Amanda pays $750 for a table and five matching chairs. If the table costs $200, how much do the chairs cost?

57. Beth saved $500 in January. She saved $350 in February. She needed to save $1,000 by March. How much did Beth have to save in March?

Singapore Math Practice Level 3B

58. Josie bought an electronic toy for $34.90. She gave the cashier 4 10-dollar bills. How much change should she receive?

59. After Andy spent $80.35 and Aaron spent $43.60, both had the same amount of money left.

(a) If Andy had $19.65 left, how much money did Aaron have at first?

(b) How much more money did Andy have than Aaron?

Singapore Math Practice Level 3B

# Unit 11: LENGTH, MASS, AND VOLUME

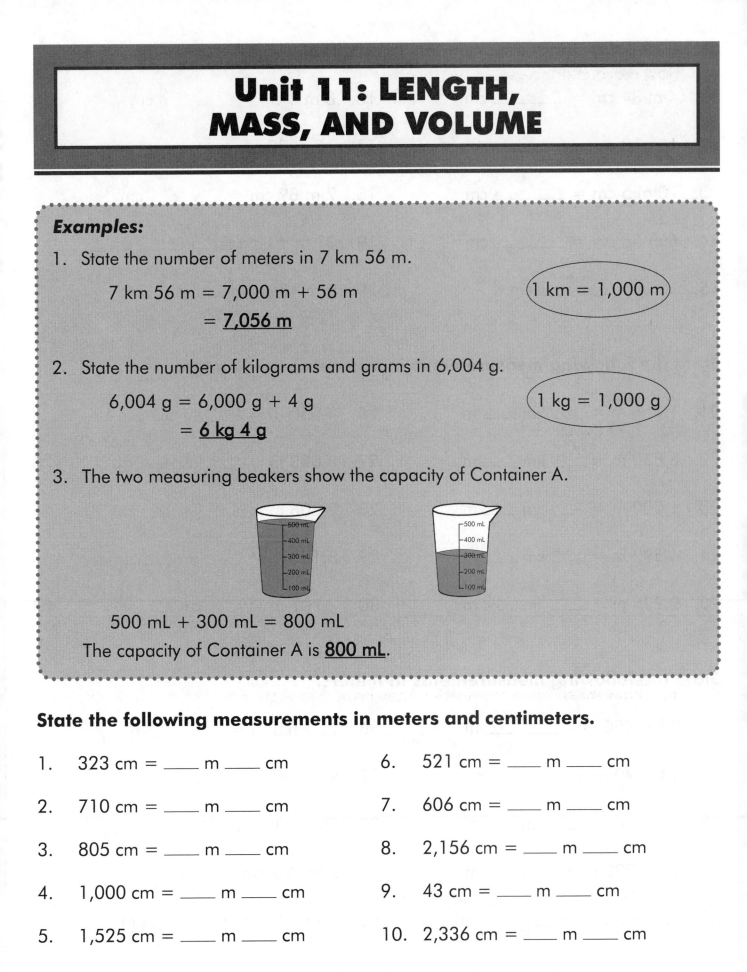

**Examples:**

1. State the number of meters in 7 km 56 m.

    7 km 56 m = 7,000 m + 56 m

    = __7,056 m__

    $\boxed{1 \text{ km} = 1,000 \text{ m}}$

2. State the number of kilograms and grams in 6,004 g.

    6,004 g = 6,000 g + 4 g

    = __6 kg 4 g__

    $\boxed{1 \text{ kg} = 1,000 \text{ g}}$

3. The two measuring beakers show the capacity of Container A.

    500 mL + 300 mL = 800 mL

    The capacity of Container A is __800 mL__.

## State the following measurements in meters and centimeters.

1.  323 cm = ___ m ___ cm

2.  710 cm = ___ m ___ cm

3.  805 cm = ___ m ___ cm

4.  1,000 cm = ___ m ___ cm

5.  1,525 cm = ___ m ___ cm

6.  521 cm = ___ m ___ cm

7.  606 cm = ___ m ___ cm

8.  2,156 cm = ___ m ___ cm

9.  43 cm = ___ m ___ cm

10. 2,336 cm = ___ m ___ cm

23

## State the following measurements in centimeters.

11.  4 m 34 cm = _____ cm

12.  1 m 10 cm = _____ cm

13.  10 m 5 cm = _____ cm

14.  6 m 56 cm = _____ cm

15.  20 m = _____ cm

16.  8 m 8 cm = _____ cm

17.  15 m 30 cm = _____ cm

18.  7 m 89 cm = _____ cm

19.  31 m 40 cm = _____ cm

20.  9 m 45 cm = _____ cm

## State the following measurements in kilometers and meters.

21.  1,456 m = ____ km ____ m

22.  6,830 m = ____ km ____ m

23.  1,000 m = ____ km ____ m

24.  6,592 m = ____ km ____ m

25.  9,225 m = ____ km ____ m

26.  4,050 m = ____ km ____ m

27.  8,003 m = ____ km ____ m

28.  2,006 m = ____ km ____ m

29.  3,100 m = ____ km ____ m

30.  7,707 m = ____ km ____ m

## State the following measurements in meters.

31.  3 km 850 m = _____ m

32.  1 km 70 m = _____ m

33.  5 km = _____ m

34.  9 km 220 m = _____ m

35.  12 km 500 m = _____ m

36.  27 km 3 m = _____ m

37.  9 km 90 m = _____ m

38.  20 km 100 m = _____ m

39.  2 km 300 m = _____ m

40.  1 km 309 m = _____ m

**Study the map below and answer the following questions.**

41.

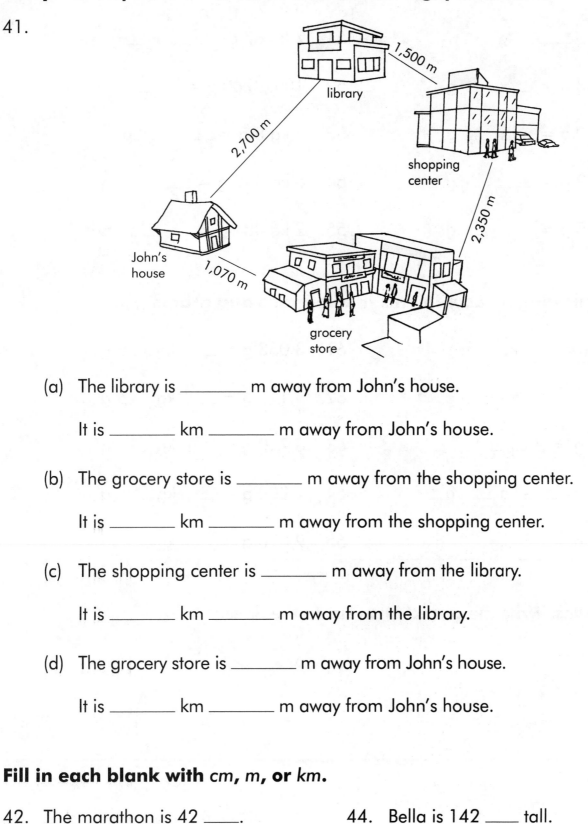

library

1,500 m

2,700 m

shopping
center

2,350 m

John's
house

1,070 m

grocery
store

(a) The library is _____ m away from John's house.

It is _____ km _____ m away from John's house.

(b) The grocery store is _____ m away from the shopping center.

It is _____ km _____ m away from the shopping center.

(c) The shopping center is _____ m away from the library.

It is _____ km _____ m away from the library.

(d) The grocery store is _____ m away from John's house.

It is _____ km _____ m away from John's house.

**Fill in each blank with cm, m, or km.**

42. The marathon is 42 ____.

43. The pencil is 15 ____.

44. Bella is 142 ____ tall.

45. The tree is 1 ____ tall.

**25**

Singapore Math Practice Level 3B

## State the following measurements in grams.

46. 1 kg = _____ g

47. 1 kg 238 g = _____ g

48. 3 kg 300 g = _____ g

49. 9 kg 569 g = _____ g

50. 5 kg 955 g = _____ g

51. 7 kg 67 g = _____ g

52. 10 kg 760 g = _____ g

53. 4 kg 8 g = _____ g

54. 8 kg 642 g = _____ g

55. 2 kg 484 g = _____ g

## State the following measurements in kilograms and grams.

56. 1,369 g = ____ kg ____ g

57. 4,820 g = ____ kg ____ g

58. 12,790 g = ____ kg ____ g

59. 6,606 g = ____ kg ____ g

60. 10,001 g = ____ kg ____ g

61. 3,033 g = ____ kg ____ g

62. 5,115 g = ____ kg ____ g

63. 8,780 g = ____ kg ____ g

64. 2,200 g = ____ kg ____ g

65. 9,090 g = ____ kg ____ g

## Read the scales. Write the correct answers on the lines.

66.

67.

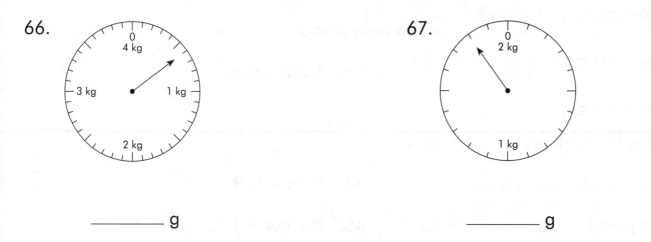

_____ g

_____ g

Singapore Math Practice Level 3B

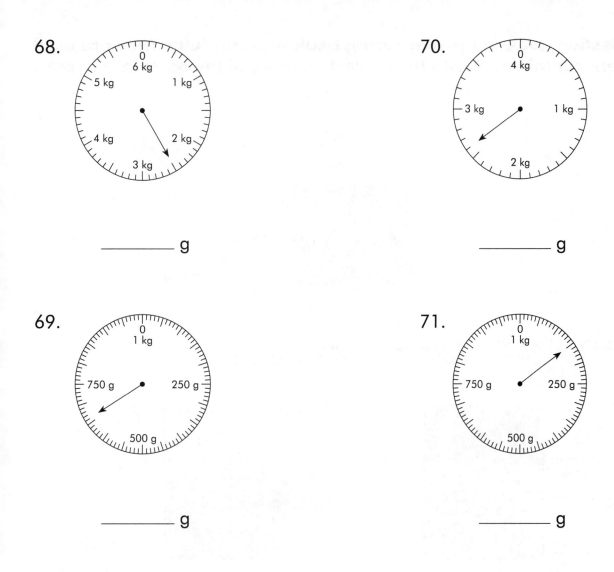

68. _____ g

70. _____ g

69. _____ g

71. _____ g

**Fill in each blank with g or kg.**

72. The mass of an apple is 180 _____.

73. The mass of David is 29 _____.

74. The mass of an elephant is 5,000 _____.

75. The mass of a book is 325 _____.

**For each question, look at the measuring beaker(s) carefully. They are used to fill different containers. Write the correct capacity of the container in each blank.**

76.

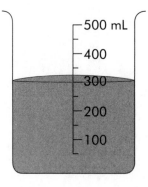

The capacity of the container is _____ mL.

77.

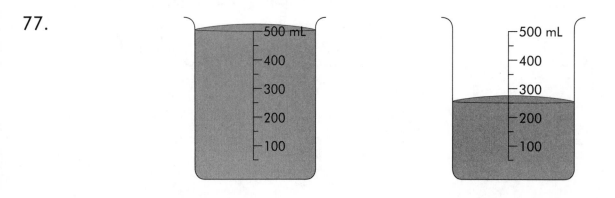

The capacity of the container is _____ mL.

78.

The capacity of the container is _____ L _____ mL.

Singapore Math Practice Level 3B

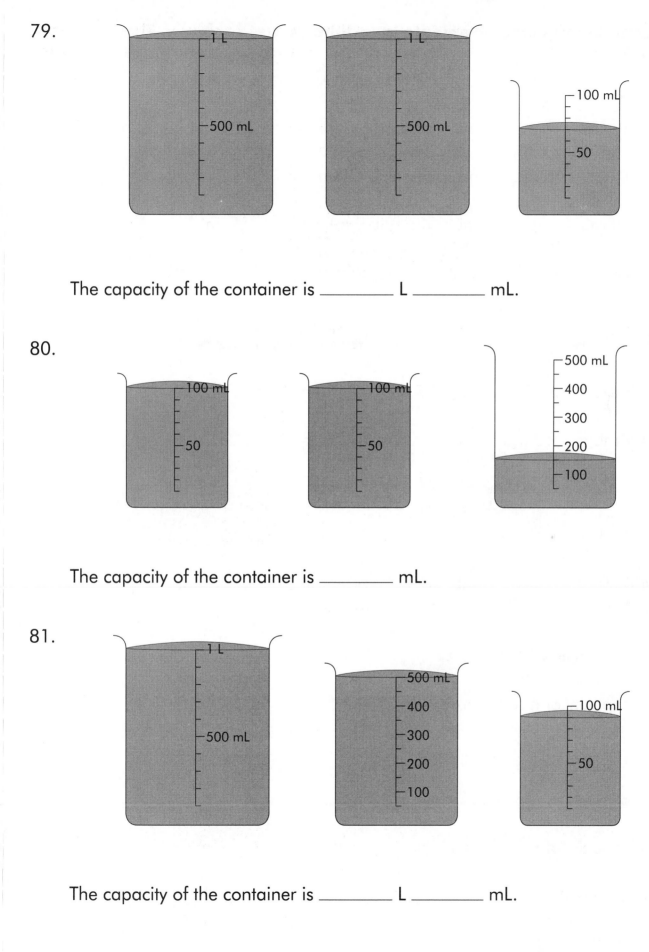

79.

The capacity of the container is _____ L _____ mL.

80.

The capacity of the container is _____ mL.

81.

The capacity of the container is _____ L _____ mL.

## State the following measurements in milliliters.

82.  1 L = _____ mL

87.  3 L 8 mL = _____ mL

83.  4 L 368 mL = _____ mL

88.  8 L 96 mL = _____ mL

84.  10 L 10 mL = _____ mL

89.  7 L 478 mL = _____ mL

85.  8 L 818 mL = _____ mL

90.  9 L 9 mL = _____ mL

86.  12 L 200 mL = _____ mL

91.  11 L 110 mL = _____ mL

## State the following measurements in liters and milliliters.

92.  4,352 mL = ____ L ____ mL

97.  5,015 mL = ____ L ____ mL

93.  9,909 mL = ____ L ____ mL

98.  7,007 mL = ____ L ____ mL

94.  3,100 mL = ____ L ____ mL

99.  6,060 mL = ____ L ____ mL

95.  8,702 mL = ____ L ____ mL

100. 10,001 mL = ____ L ____ mL

96.  2,000 mL = ____ L ____ mL

101. 1,100 mL = ____ L ____ mL

## Fill in each blank with *mL* or *L.*

102.  The capacity of a soft drink can is 325 ____.

103.  The capacity of a crockpot is 2 ____.

104.  The capacity of a bottle of water is 500 ____.

105.  The capacity of a fish tank is 10 ____.

Singapore Math Practice Level 3B

# Unit 12: PROBLEM SOLVING (LENGTH, MASS, AND VOLUME)

**Examples:**

1. Jose draws 5 buckets of water from a well. He fills each bucket to the brim with water. The capacity of each bucket is 3 L. How many liters of water does Jose draw from the well?

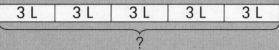

$5 \times 3 = 15$

Jose draws **15 L** of water from the well.

2. The distance between Greenland Mall and Sunshine Fitness Center is 1 km 250 m. The distance between the library and Sunshine Fitness Center is 1 km 50 m. Rafi walks from Greenland Mall, past the Sunshine Fitness Center, to the library. After borrowing books from the library, he walks back to Sunshine Fitness Center. What is the total distance Rafi has walked?

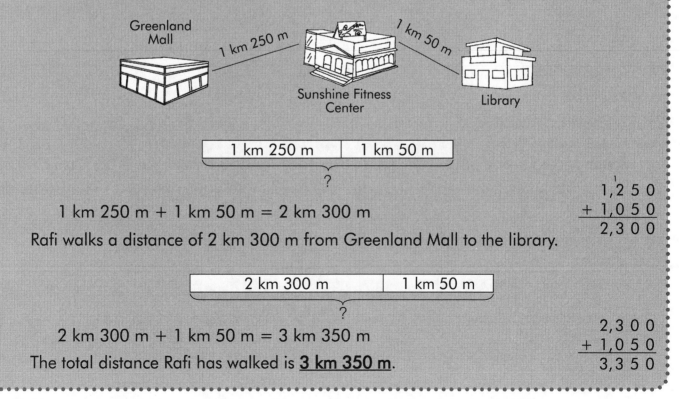

1 km 250 m + 1 km 50 m = 2 km 300 m

Rafi walks a distance of 2 km 300 m from Greenland Mall to the library.

$$\begin{array}{r} 1,\!2\,5\,0 \\ +\ 1,\!0\,5\,0 \\ \hline 2,\!3\,0\,0 \end{array}$$

2 km 300 m + 1 km 50 m = 3 km 350 m

The total distance Rafi has walked is **3 km 350 m**.

$$\begin{array}{r} 2,\!3\,0\,0 \\ +\ 1,\!0\,5\,0 \\ \hline 3,\!3\,5\,0 \end{array}$$

Singapore Math Practice Level 3B

**Solve the following story problems. Show your work in the space below.**

1.  A pole is longer than a wooden plank by 88 cm. If the pole is 325 cm, what is the length of the wooden plank?

2.  A ribbon 840 cm long is cut into 5 equal pieces. What is the length of each piece of ribbon?

3.  Jonah's mass is 38 kg and Haruka's mass is 37 kg. What is their total mass?

4.  Sarah mixed some flour with butter. The mixture had a mass of 3,000 g. If she used 900 g of butter, how much flour did she use? State your answer in kilograms and grams.

Singapore Math Practice Level 3B

5.  Mandy prepares 10,360 mL of latte. If she uses 7,900 mL of coffee, how much milk does she add?

6.  Sharon's car has a tank capacity of 40 L. How much gasoline has she used up if there are 18 L of gasoline left in her tank? Assume that she fills her car up with gasoline every time.

7.  Ms. Drew bought a box of crackers. The mass of the box of crackers was 1,800 g. She packed the crackers into 3 equal bags. What was the mass of each bag of crackers?

8.  Grace bought a dozen similar cans of orange juice. If the capacity of each can of orange juice was 550 mL, how much orange juice did she buy? State your answer in liters and milliliters.

33

9. The total length of three sticks is 555 cm. If two of the sticks measure a total of 272 cm, what is the length of the third stick? State your answer in meters and centimeters.

10. A chair has a mass of 2,700 g. A table has a mass of 3,960 g. How much heavier is the table than the chair?

11. The length of a garden is 8 m and its width is 6 m. If John wants to put up a fence around the garden, how long will the fence be?

12. Basir's bag of groceries has a mass of 4,870 g. His bag of groceries is 3,560 g heavier than Andy's. What is the mass of Andy and Basir's bags of groceries? State your answer in kilograms and grams.

13. A fish market sold 30,960 g of fish on Saturday. It sold 10,040 g of fish on Sunday. How much fish did the market sell on both days? State your answer in kilograms and grams.

Singapore Math Practice Level 3B

14. Sam bought 8,300 mL of paint. Evan bought 6,970 mL less of paint. How much paint did they buy altogether?

15. Kelly used 125 g of flour to make pastries. Her sister used 5 times as much flour to bake cakes. How much more flour did her sister use than Kelly? State your answer in grams.

16. Tree A is 135 cm. Tree B is 3 times taller than Tree A. What is the total height of both trees?

17. Andre has to paint a wall of 15 m by 3 m. Tim has to paint another wall of 12 m by 4 m.

    (a) Who has to paint more wall space?

    (b) How much more wall space does he have to paint?

18.

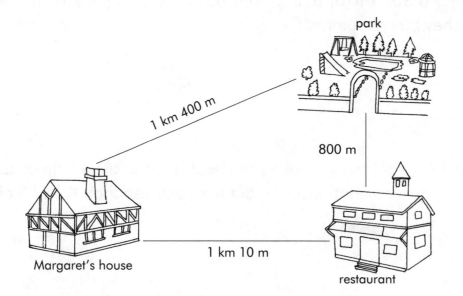

park

1 km 400 m

800 m

Margaret's house

1 km 10 m

restaurant

Margaret walked from her house to the park and then to the restaurant. She then walked home from the restaurant. What was the total distance walked by Margaret? State your answer in kilometers and meters.

19. Jake uses 6,500 mL of water on Monday. His brother uses 2,765 mL of water more than Jake. How much water do both of them use? State your answer in liters and milliliters.

20. Joshua poured a bottle of milk into 8 glasses and had a remaining 250 mL of milk.

    (a)    If each glass of milk had a volume of 420 mL, find the total volume of the 8 glasses of milk.

    (b)    How much milk was there in all? State your answer in liters and milliliters.

21. A waiter filled some pots of coffee to the brim. Each pot could hold 2 L of coffee.

    (a)    If the waiter had 14 L of coffee, how many pots of coffee could he fill?

    (b)    If the waiter had 2 pots of coffee left after breakfast, how many pots of coffee were used?

# REVIEW 1

**Fill in each blank with the correct answer.**

1. (a) 415 cm = _____ m _____ cm    (b) 830 cm = _____ m _____ cm

2. (a) 6,269 m = _____ km _____ m    (b) 5,500 m = _____ km _____ m

3. (a) 7,670 g = _____ kg _____ g    (b) 4,008 g = _____ kg _____ g

4. (a) 4,835 mL = _____ L _____ mL    (b) 6,505 ml = _____ L _____ mL

5. (a) 6 km 975 m = _____ m    (b) 8 km 8 m = _____ m

6. (a) 9 m 5 cm = _____ cm    (b) 10 m = _____ cm

7. (a) 2 L 2 mL = _____ mL    (b) 5 L 275 mL = _____ mL

8. (a) 2 kg 636 g = _____ g    (b) 5 kg 30 g = _____ g

9.

The mass of a watermelon is _____ g.

10.

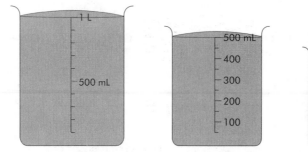

The capacity of a water bottle is _____ mL.

Singapore Math Practice Level 3B

11. Below are some items sold at a bakery.

(a) Angie buys a loaf of bread and a piece of cake. How much does she pay altogether?

$_____

(b) Samantha buys 2 buns. She gives the cashier $5. How much change will she receive?

$_____

(c) Tony buys four 1-kg cakes and a doughnut. How much does he pay in all?

$_____

12. Study the map below carefully and answer the following questions.

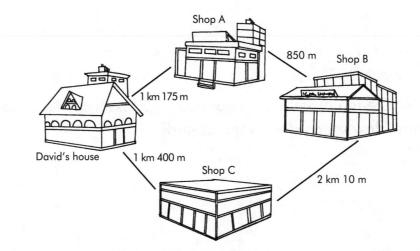

(a) Shop A is _____ m away from Shop B.

(b) Shop C is _____ m away from David's house.

(c) The distance between David's house and Shop A is _____ m.

Singapore Math Practice Level 3B

**Solve the following story problems. Show your work in the space below.**

13. Ken gives $500 of his salary to his parents. He spends $375 and saves the rest. If he earns $1,200 every month, how much does Ken save?

14. Benjamin jogs twice daily. He jogs a distance of 8 km 120 m each time. How far does Benjamin jog daily? Write your answer in kilometers and meters.

15. Alex spends $410 each month. Sam spends $75 less than Alex. John spends $160 more than Sam. How much does John spend?

Singapore Math Practice Level 3B

16. Greg mixes 4 kg 360 g of cement with 2 kg 500 g of sand.

    (a) How much more cement does he mix? Write your answer in kilograms and grams.

    (b) What is the total mass of the mixture? Write your answer in kilograms and grams.

17. The total length of two poles is 5 m 70 cm. Pole A is 2 m 25 cm long.

    (a) Which pole is longer, A or B?

    (b) How much longer? Write your answer in centimeters.

Singapore Math Practice Level 3B

18. Zoe bought four cartons of milk. If each carton of milk was 250 mL, what was the total volume of the four cartons of milk? Write your answer in liters.

19. Sam pays $10.00 for some oranges, apples, and pears. If the apples cost $3.60 and the pears cost $3.55, how much do the oranges cost?

20. Mandy made 3 L 250 mL of orange juice on Monday. She made 1,670 mL of orange juice on Tuesday. If she poured the orange juice equally into 6 containers, how much orange juice was there in each container?

# Unit 13: BAR GRAPHS

**Example:**

Mr. Ford sells technology products in his store. He recorded the sales of these products for the month of February in the bar graph below. Study the bar graph carefully and answer the questions.

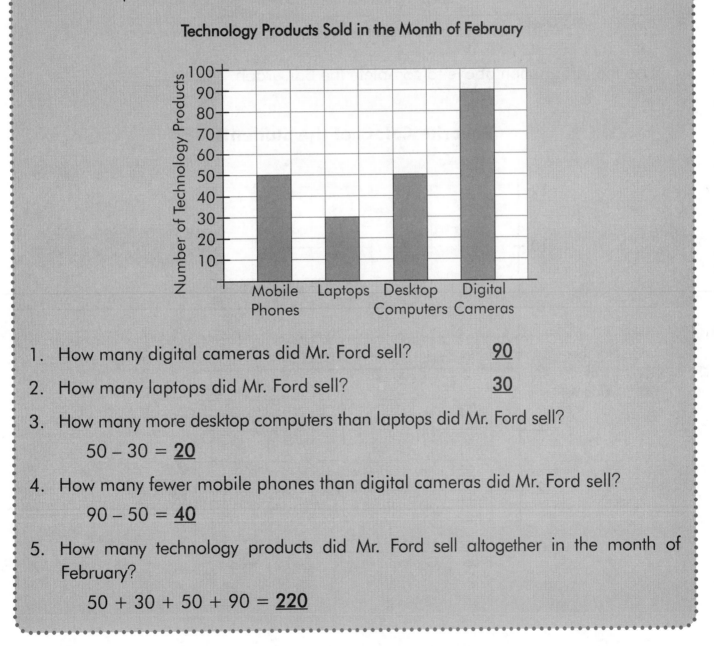

Technology Products Sold in the Month of February

1.  How many digital cameras did Mr. Ford sell?          **90**

2.  How many laptops did Mr. Ford sell?          **30**

3.  How many more desktop computers than laptops did Mr. Ford sell?

    50 – 30 = **20**

4.  How many fewer mobile phones than digital cameras did Mr. Ford sell?

    90 – 50 = **40**

5.  How many technology products did Mr. Ford sell altogether in the month of February?

    50 + 30 + 50 + 90 = **220**

**43**

1. The picture graph below shows the favorite colors of a class of 40 students.

| blue | ★ ★ ★ ★ ★ ★ ★ ★ ★ ★ ★ ★ |
|---|---|
| green | ★ ★ ★ ★ ★ ★ |
| purple | ★ ★ ★ ★ ★ ★ ★ ★ ★ |
| red | ★ ★ ★ ★ ★ ★ ★ ★ |
| yellow | ★ ★ ★ ★ ★ ★ |
| | Each ★ stands for 1 student. |

Use the information above to complete the bar graph.

**Favorite Colors of the Students**

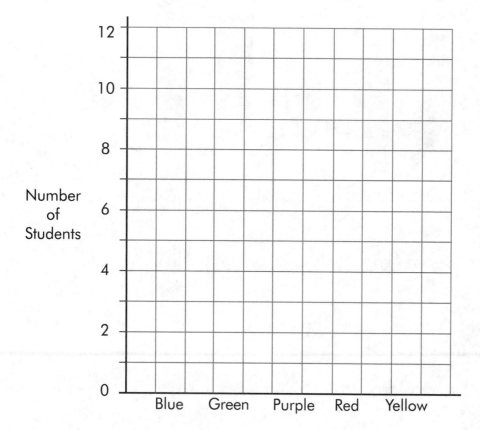

Singapore Math Practice Level 3B

2. The picture graph below shows the number of adults at different booths during a travel exhibition.

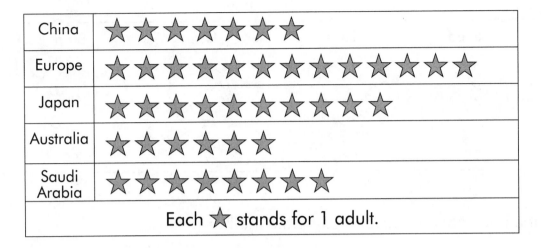

| China | ★ ★ ★ ★ ★ ★ ★ |
| Europe | ★ ★ ★ ★ ★ ★ ★ ★ ★ ★ ★ ★ |
| Japan | ★ ★ ★ ★ ★ ★ ★ ★ ★ ★ |
| Australia | ★ ★ ★ ★ ★ |
| Saudi Arabia | ★ ★ ★ ★ ★ ★ ★ ★ |

Each ★ stands for 1 adult.

Use the information above to complete the bar graph.

**Number of Adults at Different Booths**

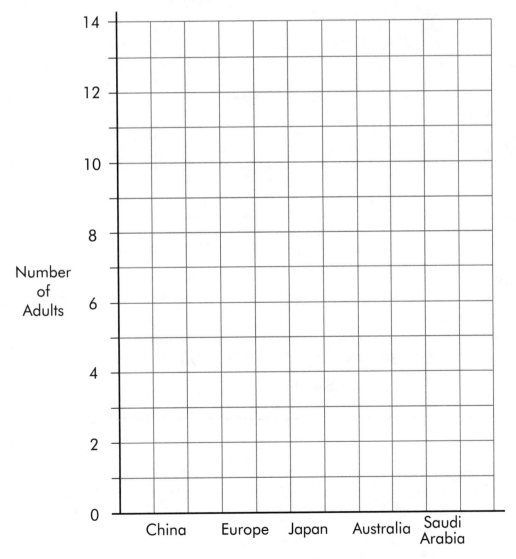

Singapore Math Practice Level 3B

3. Justin and his friends played a board game. The points scored by the four boys are shown below.

| Akmed | Luke | Justin | Brad |
|-------|------|--------|------|
| 95 | 80 | 75 | 65 |

Use the information above to complete the bar graph.

**Points Scored**

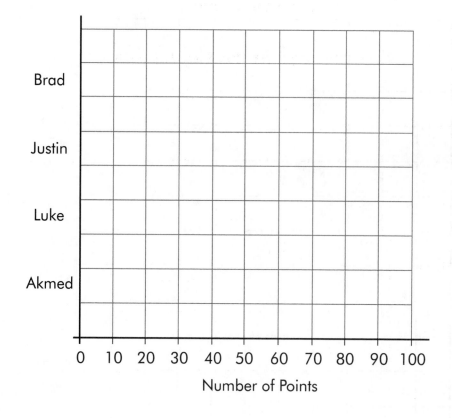

Number of Points

Singapore Math Practice Level 3B

4. Mrs. Jones works at a dry cleaners. The number of pieces of laundry cleaned in a day is shown below.

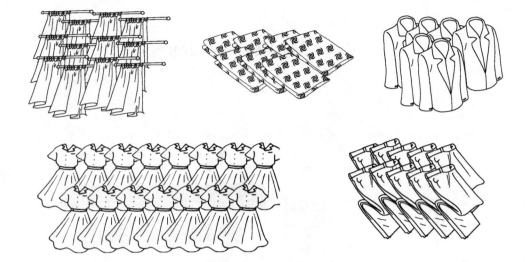

Use the information to complete the bar graph.

## Items Cleaned at the Dry Cleaners

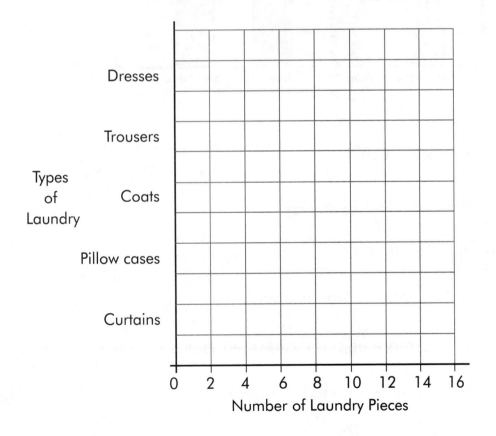

Singapore Math Practice Level 3B

5.  A fruit seller sold some fruit on Sunday. He recorded the number of pieces he sold in the bar graph below. Study the bar graph carefully and fill in each blank with the correct answer.

**Fruit Sold on Sunday**

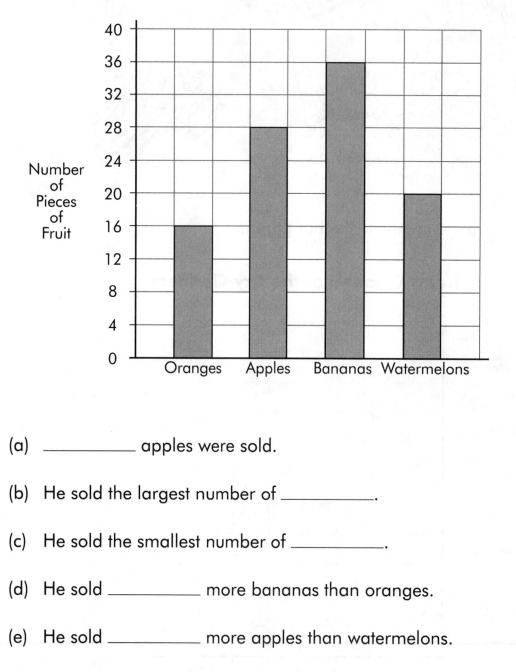

(a)  _____ apples were sold.

(b)  He sold the largest number of _____.

(c)  He sold the smallest number of _____.

(d)  He sold _____ more bananas than oranges.

(e)  He sold _____ more apples than watermelons.

(f)  The total number of fruit sold on that Sunday was _____.

Singapore Math Practice Level 3B

6.  Ana and her sister went to a park. They drew a bar graph of what they saw at the park. Study the bar graph carefully and fill in each blank with the correct answer.

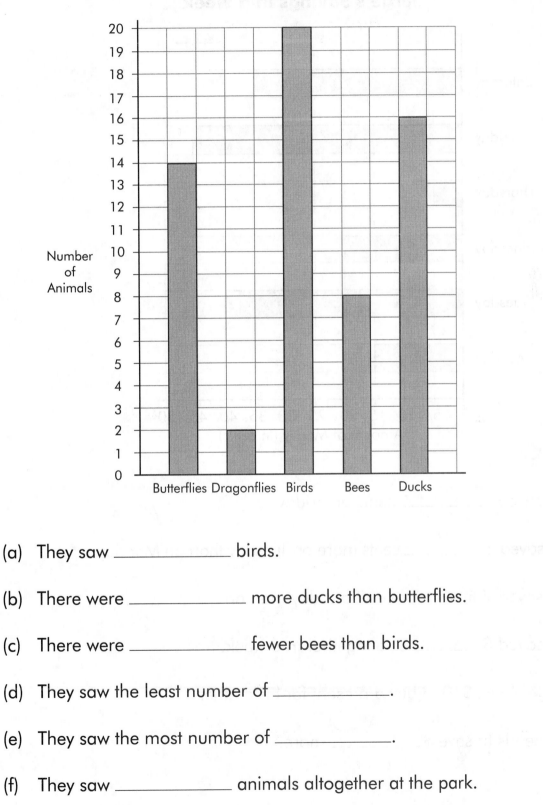

**Animals at a Park**

(a) They saw _____ birds.

(b) There were _____ more ducks than butterflies.

(c) There were _____ fewer bees than birds.

(d) They saw the least number of _____.

(e) They saw the most number of _____.

(f) They saw _____ animals altogether at the park.

Singapore Math Practice Level 3B

7. Jorge saved some money in a week. He recorded the amount of money he saved in the bar graph below. Study the bar graph carefully and fill in each blank with the correct answer.

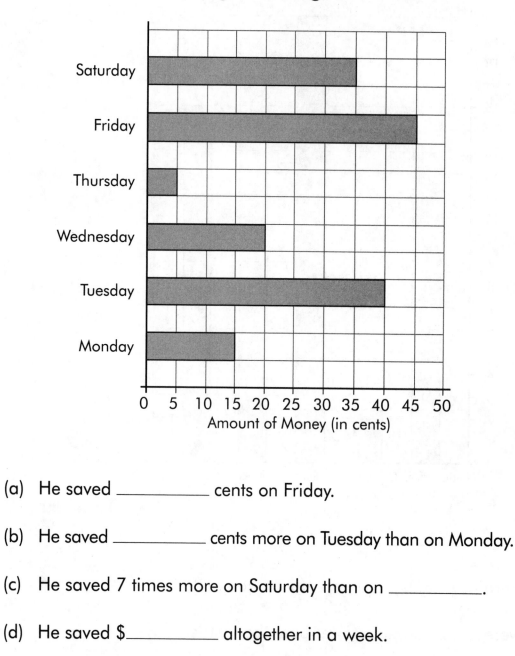

**Jorge's Savings in a Week**

(a) He saved _____ cents on Friday.

(b) He saved _____ cents more on Tuesday than on Monday.

(c) He saved 7 times more on Saturday than on _____.

(d) He saved $_____ altogether in a week.

(e) Jorge needs $10 to buy a present for his mother.

He needs to save $_____ more.

Singapore Math Practice Level 3B

8. The bar graph below illustrates the different types of instruments played by the students in a music school. Study the bar graph carefully and fill in each blank with the correct answer.

**Instruments Played in a Music School**

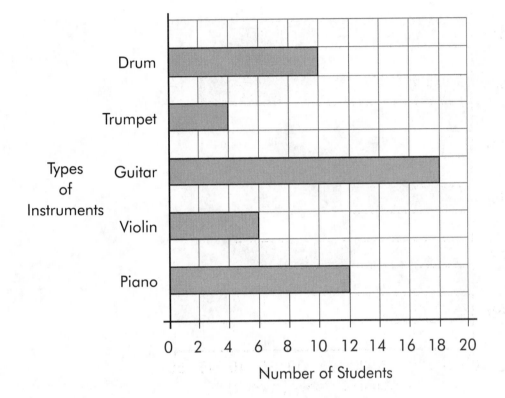

(a) _____ students play violin.

(b) _____ students play drum.

(c) _____ more students play guitar than trumpet.

(d) _____ fewer students play piano than guitar.

(e) There are _____ students in the music school.

Singapore Math Practice Level 3B

# Unit 14: FRACTIONS

**Examples:**

1. Find the equivalent fractions.

$$\frac{2}{3} = \frac{\boxed{6}}{9} = \frac{8}{\boxed{12}}$$

$$\frac{2 \times 3}{3 \times 3} = \frac{6}{9}$$

$$\frac{2 \times 4}{3 \times 4} = \frac{8}{12}$$

2. Which fraction is smaller, $\frac{5}{6}$ or $\frac{3}{12}$?

$$\frac{5 \times 2}{6 \times 2} = \frac{10}{12}$$

The smaller fraction is $\frac{3}{12}$.

3. Add $\frac{1}{8}$ and $\frac{1}{4}$.

$$\frac{1 \times 2}{4 \times 2} = \frac{2}{8}$$

$$\frac{1}{8} + \frac{2}{8} = \frac{3}{8}$$

4. What is $1 - \frac{2}{9} - \frac{2}{3}$?

$$1 = \frac{9}{9}$$

$$\frac{2 \times 3}{3 \times 3} = \frac{6}{9}$$

$$\frac{9}{9} - \frac{2}{9} - \frac{6}{9} = \frac{1}{9}$$

Singapore Math Practice Level 3B

# Study the following diagrams. Fill in each box with the correct answer.

1.

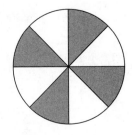

$$\frac{4}{\boxed{\phantom{0}}}$$

2.

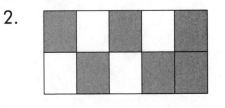

$$\frac{6}{\boxed{\phantom{0}}}$$

3.

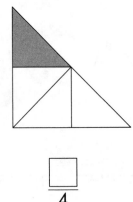

$$\frac{\boxed{\phantom{0}}}{4}$$

4.

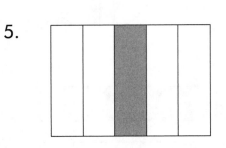

$$\frac{\boxed{\phantom{0}}}{9}$$

5.

$$\frac{1}{\boxed{\phantom{0}}}$$

Singapore Math Practice Level 3B

**Shade the correct parts to show the equivalent fraction. Write the equivalent fraction in the boxes provided.**

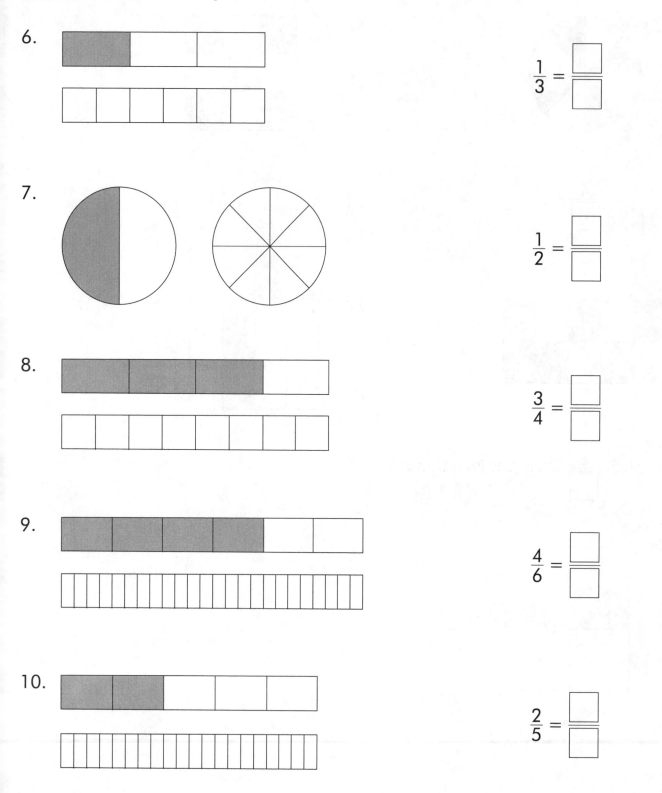

6.

$$\frac{1}{3} = \frac{\boxed{\phantom{0}}}{\boxed{\phantom{0}}}$$

7.

$$\frac{1}{2} = \frac{\boxed{\phantom{0}}}{\boxed{\phantom{0}}}$$

8.

$$\frac{3}{4} = \frac{\boxed{\phantom{0}}}{\boxed{\phantom{0}}}$$

9.

$$\frac{4}{6} = \frac{\boxed{\phantom{0}}}{\boxed{\phantom{0}}}$$

10.

$$\frac{2}{5} = \frac{\boxed{\phantom{0}}}{\boxed{\phantom{0}}}$$

Singapore Math Practice Level 3B

**Fill in each box with the correct answer to make the equivalent fraction.**

11. $\dfrac{2}{3} = \dfrac{\boxed{\phantom{0}}}{9}$

12. $\dfrac{4}{8} = \dfrac{20}{\boxed{\phantom{0}}}$

13. $\dfrac{3}{7} = \dfrac{\boxed{\phantom{0}}}{28}$

14. $\dfrac{1}{10} = \dfrac{8}{\boxed{\phantom{0}}}$

15. $\dfrac{5}{9} = \dfrac{35}{\boxed{\phantom{0}}}$

16. $\dfrac{3}{4} = \dfrac{12}{\boxed{\phantom{0}}}$

17. $\dfrac{7}{12} = \dfrac{\boxed{\phantom{0}}}{36}$

18. $\dfrac{2}{6} = \dfrac{\boxed{\phantom{0}}}{36}$

19. $\dfrac{6}{11} = \dfrac{42}{\boxed{\phantom{0}}}$

20. $\dfrac{3}{5} = \dfrac{\boxed{\phantom{0}}}{30}$

**List all of the equivalent fractions.**

21. $\dfrac{1}{5} = \dfrac{\boxed{\phantom{0}}}{10} = \dfrac{3}{\boxed{\phantom{0}}} = \dfrac{4}{\boxed{\phantom{0}}} = \dfrac{5}{\boxed{\phantom{0}}}$

22. $\dfrac{3}{8} = \dfrac{\boxed{\phantom{0}}}{16} = \dfrac{\boxed{\phantom{0}}}{24} = \dfrac{12}{\boxed{\phantom{0}}} = \dfrac{15}{\boxed{\phantom{0}}}$

23. $\dfrac{2}{5} = \dfrac{4}{\boxed{\phantom{0}}} = \dfrac{\boxed{\phantom{0}}}{15} = \dfrac{8}{\boxed{\phantom{0}}} = \dfrac{10}{\boxed{\phantom{0}}}$

24. $\dfrac{1}{4} = \dfrac{2}{\boxed{\phantom{0}}} = \dfrac{\boxed{\phantom{0}}}{12} = \dfrac{4}{\boxed{\phantom{0}}} = \dfrac{5}{\boxed{\phantom{0}}}$

Singapore Math Practice Level 3B

25. $\dfrac{1}{7} = \dfrac{\boxed{\phantom{0}}}{14} = \dfrac{\boxed{\phantom{0}}}{21} = \dfrac{4}{\boxed{\phantom{0}}} = \dfrac{5}{\boxed{\phantom{0}}}$

## Write each fraction in its simplest form.

26. $\dfrac{7}{21} = \dfrac{\boxed{\phantom{0}}}{\boxed{\phantom{0}}}$

27. $\dfrac{3}{9} = \dfrac{\boxed{\phantom{0}}}{\boxed{\phantom{0}}}$

28. $\dfrac{8}{16} = \dfrac{\boxed{\phantom{0}}}{\boxed{\phantom{0}}}$

29. $\dfrac{36}{45} = \dfrac{\boxed{\phantom{0}}}{\boxed{\phantom{0}}}$

30. $\dfrac{35}{42} = \dfrac{\boxed{\phantom{0}}}{\boxed{\phantom{0}}}$

31. $\dfrac{9}{63} = \dfrac{\boxed{\phantom{0}}}{\boxed{\phantom{0}}}$

32. $\dfrac{44}{66} = \dfrac{\boxed{\phantom{0}}}{\boxed{\phantom{0}}}$

33. $\dfrac{64}{72} = \dfrac{\boxed{\phantom{0}}}{\boxed{\phantom{0}}}$

34. $\dfrac{12}{18} = \dfrac{\boxed{\phantom{0}}}{\boxed{\phantom{0}}}$

35. $\dfrac{9}{24} = \dfrac{\boxed{\phantom{0}}}{\boxed{\phantom{0}}}$

## Fill in each blank with the correct fraction.

36.

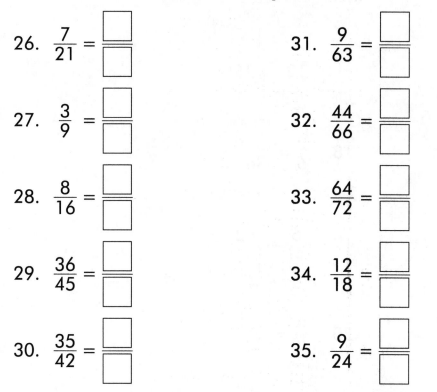

_____ is greater than _____.

37.

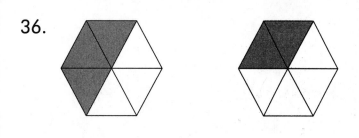

_____ is smaller than _____.

Singapore Math Practice Level 3B

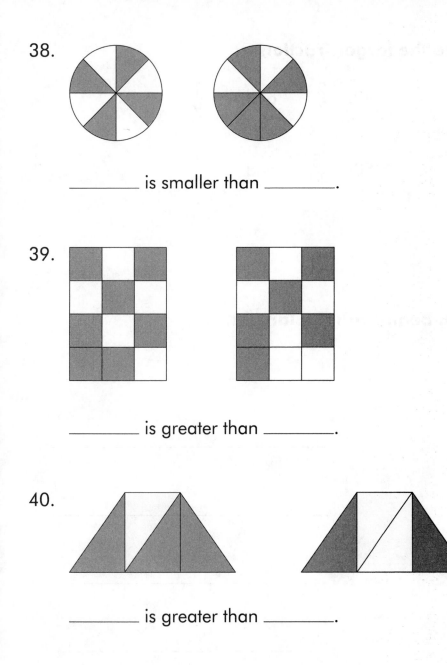

38. 

_____ is smaller than _____.

39. 

_____ is greater than _____.

40. 

_____ is greater than _____.

## Compare these fractions. Circle the smaller fraction.

41. $\frac{1}{6}$    and    $\frac{5}{6}$

42. $\frac{4}{9}$    and    $\frac{2}{9}$

43. $\frac{3}{6}$    and    $\frac{3}{9}$

44. $\frac{5}{8}$    and    $\frac{5}{11}$

45. $\frac{7}{12}$    and    $\frac{7}{9}$

**Compare these fractions. Circle the larger fraction.**

46. $\frac{2}{3}$   and   $\frac{6}{12}$

47. $\frac{3}{8}$   and   $\frac{2}{5}$

48. $\frac{4}{6}$   and   $\frac{2}{8}$

49. $\frac{2}{7}$   and   $\frac{1}{9}$

50. $\frac{3}{11}$   and   $\frac{1}{4}$

**Arrange the fractions in order. Begin with the largest.**

51. $\frac{3}{9}, \frac{8}{9}, \frac{5}{9}$  _____

52. $\frac{4}{6}, \frac{2}{8}, \frac{3}{4}$  _____

53. $\frac{7}{12}, \frac{3}{4}, \frac{1}{6}$  _____

54. $\frac{2}{5}, \frac{8}{9}, \frac{4}{15}$  _____

55. $\frac{6}{7}, \frac{6}{12}, \frac{6}{9}$  _____

**Arrange the fractions in order. Begin with the smallest.**

56. $\frac{2}{3}, \frac{2}{5}, \frac{2}{4}$  _____

57. $\frac{3}{8}, \frac{4}{6}, \frac{1}{4}$  _____

58. $\frac{6}{10}, \frac{3}{6}, \frac{1}{5}$  _____

Singapore Math Practice Level 3B

59. $\dfrac{12}{20}, \dfrac{18}{20}, \dfrac{11}{20}$ _____

60. $\dfrac{4}{7}, \dfrac{5}{6}, \dfrac{2}{3}$ _____

## Add these fractions.

61. $\dfrac{2}{3} + \dfrac{1}{9} =$

62. $\dfrac{1}{4} + \dfrac{1}{2} =$

63. $\dfrac{5}{12} + \dfrac{1}{6} =$

64. $\dfrac{2}{5} + \dfrac{3}{10} =$

65. $\dfrac{3}{8} + \dfrac{1}{4} =$

## Subtract these fractions.

66. $\dfrac{1}{2} - \dfrac{1}{5} =$

67. $\dfrac{4}{5} - \dfrac{7}{10} =$

68. $\dfrac{7}{8} - \dfrac{3}{4} =$

69. $\dfrac{5}{6} - \dfrac{5}{12} =$

70. $\dfrac{4}{9} - \dfrac{1}{3} =$

**Solve the problems below. Write the correct answers on the lines.**

71. Find the sum of $\frac{1}{9}$, $\frac{1}{3}$, and $\frac{4}{9}$.  _____

72. Find the sum of $\frac{1}{4}$, $\frac{3}{8}$, and $\frac{1}{8}$.  _____

73. Find $1 - \frac{7}{12} - \frac{1}{6}$.  _____

74. Find $1 - \frac{1}{3} - \frac{5}{9}$.  _____

75. What is $\frac{3}{10} + \frac{1}{2} + \frac{1}{10}$?  _____

76. What is $\frac{2}{6} + \frac{1}{3} + \frac{1}{6}$?  _____

77. What is $1 - \frac{3}{8} - \frac{1}{2}$?  _____

78. What is $1 - \frac{3}{5} - \frac{1}{10}$?  _____

Singapore Math Practice Level 3B

# Unit 15: TIME

**Examples:**

1.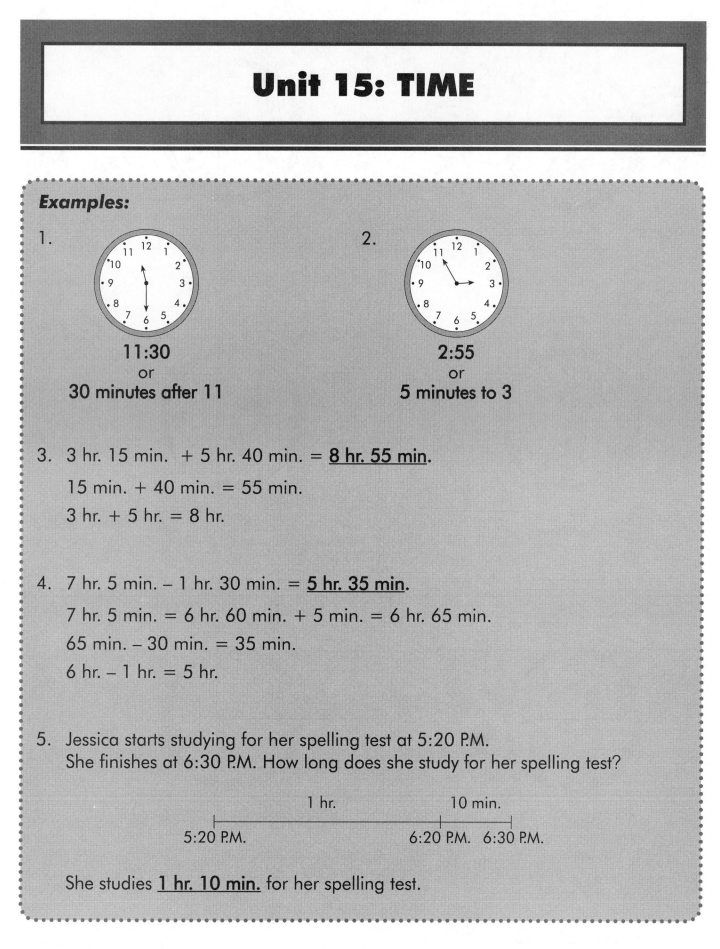

   **11:30**
   or
   **30 minutes after 11**

2. **2:55**
   or
   **5 minutes to 3**

3. 3 hr. 15 min. + 5 hr. 40 min. = **<u>8 hr. 55 min.</u>**

   15 min. + 40 min. = 55 min.

   3 hr. + 5 hr. = 8 hr.

4. 7 hr. 5 min. − 1 hr. 30 min. = **<u>5 hr. 35 min.</u>**

   7 hr. 5 min. = 6 hr. 60 min. + 5 min. = 6 hr. 65 min.

   65 min. − 30 min. = 35 min.

   6 hr. − 1 hr. = 5 hr.

5. Jessica starts studying for her spelling test at 5:20 P.M.
   She finishes at 6:30 P.M. How long does she study for her spelling test?

   |         1 hr.          |    10 min.    |
   5:20 P.M.                6:20 P.M.  6:30 P.M.

   She studies **<u>1 hr. 10 min.</u>** for her spelling test.

61

Singapore Math Practice Level 3B

# Fill in each blank with the correct time.

1.

_____

or

_____

2.

_____

or

_____

3.

_____

or

_____

4.

_____

or

_____

5.

_____

or

_____

6.

_____

or

_____

Singapore Math Practice Level 3B

7.

_____

or

_____

## Fill in each blank with the correct answer.

8. 12:25 is _____ minutes after 12.

9. 8:19 is _____ minutes after 8.

10. 4:10 is 10 minutes after _____.

11. 7:06 is 6 minutes after _____.

12. 3:55 is _____ minutes to 4.

13. 10:38 is _____ minutes to 11.

14. 5:48 is 12 minutes to _____.

15. 9:50 is 10 minutes to _____.

## State the following in minutes.

16. 3 hr. = _____ min.

17. 1 hr. 20 min. = _____ min.

18. 4 hr. 5 min. = _____ min.

19. 8 hr. 15 min. = _____ min.

20. 6 hr. 30 min. = _____ min.

Singapore Math Practice Level 3B

## State the following in hours.

21. 420 min. = _____ hr.

22. 300 min. = _____ hr.

23. 600 min. = _____ hr.

24. 240 min. = _____ hr.

25. 540 min. = _____ hr.

## State the following in hours and minutes.

26. 75 min. = ____ hr. ____ min.

27. 515 min. = ____ hr. ____ min.

28. 455 min. = ____ hr. ____ min.

29. 190 min. = ____ hr. ____ min.

30. 430 min. = ____ hr. ____ min.

## Fill in each blank with the correct answer.

31. 3 hr. 5 min. + 2 hr. 45 min. = ____ hr. ____ min.

32. 7 hr. 17 min. + 3 hr. 38 min. = ____ hr. ____ min.

33. 2 hr. 19 min. +1 hr. 39 min. = ____ hr. ____ min.

34. 5 hr. 13 min. + 2 hr. 56 min. = ____ hr. ____ min.

35. 6 hr. 28 min. + 4 hr. 50 min. = ____ hr. ____ min.

36. 8 hr. 35 min. + 1 hr. 45 min. = ____ hr. ____ min.

37. 4 hr. 50 min. – 2 hr. 30 min. = ____ hr. ____ min.

38. 10 hr. 35  min. – 7 hr. 25 min. = ____ hr. ____ min.

39. 6 hr. 30 min. – 1 hr. 5 min. = ____ hr. ____ min.

40. 8 hr. 25 min. – 3 hr. 40 min. = ____ hr. ____ min.

41. 5 hr. 15 min. – 1 hr. 45 min. = ____ hr. ____ min.

Singapore Math Practice Level 3B

42. 10 hr. 20 min. – 4 hr. 50 min. = _____ hr. _____ min.

## Draw timelines to find the length of time elapsed.

43. 4:20 P.M. to 4:50 P.M. = _____ minutes

44. 2:30 P.M. to 4:45 P.M. = _____ hours _____ minutes

45. 10:25 A.M. to 1:40 P.M. = _____ hours _____ minutes

46. 11:40 A.M. to 3:35 P.M. = _____ hours _____ minutes

47. 7:10 P.M. to 10:55 P.M. = _____ hours _____ minutes

48. 11:30 A.M. to 7:30 P.M. = _____ hours

49. 1:15 P.M. to 5:55 P.M. = _____ hours _____ minutes

Singapore Math Practice Level 3B

**Draw the correct time on the face of each clock, and write the correct time on the lines provided.**

50.

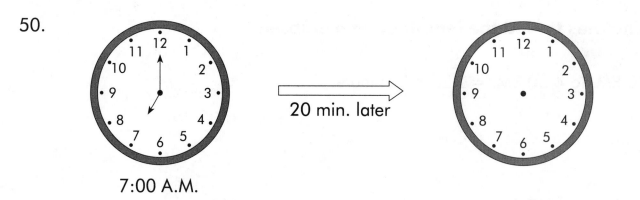

7:00 A.M.          20 min. later

_____

51.

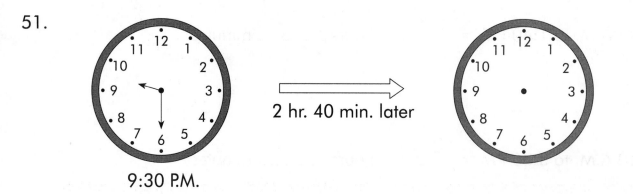

9:30 P.M.          2 hr. 40 min. later

_____

52.

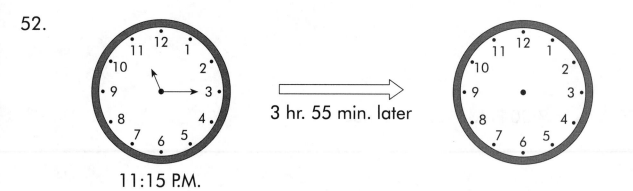

11:15 P.M.         3 hr. 55 min. later

_____

Singapore Math Practice Level 3B

53.

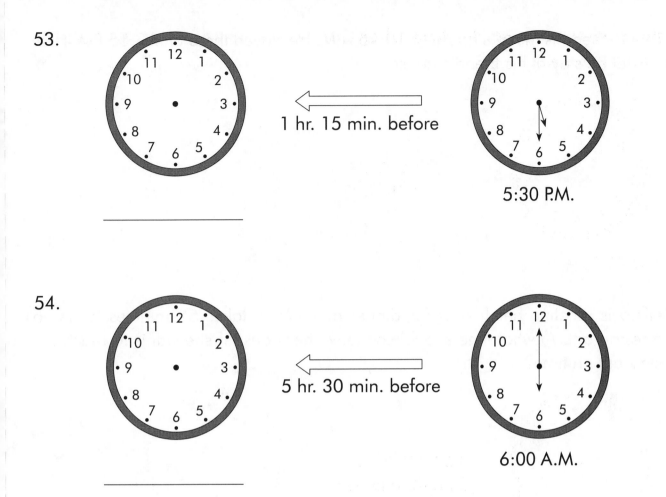

1 hr. 15 min. before

5:30 P.M.

_____

54.

5 hr. 30 min. before

6:00 A.M.

_____

**Solve the following story problems. Show your work in the space below.**

55.  Shannon and her friends watched a movie. The movie started at 5:30 P.M., and it lasted 1 hr. 20 min. What time did the movie end?

56. John reached his friend's house at 10:15 A.M. He stayed there until 2:55 P.M. How long did he stay at his friend's house?

57. Melissa is meeting her friends for dinner at 7 P.M. It takes 55 minutes to get to the restaurant. At what time should she leave her house if she wants to reach the restaurant on time?

58. Matt is a music teacher. He charges $125 an hour. The table below shows the number of hours he teaches each week. How much does Matt earn in a week?

| Days | Number of hours |
|---|---|
| Monday | 3 hr. |
| Tuesday | 2 hr. |
| Wednesday | 3 hr. |
| Thursday | 4 hr. |
| Friday | 2 hr. |
| Saturday | 5 hr. |

59. Grace works at a factory. She is paid $9 per hour. She works 8 hours every day.

(a) If she works from Monday to Friday, find the total number of hours she works in a week.

(b) How much does she earn in a week?

60. Dave is a part-time proofreader. He needs 2 hours to proofread a chapter. He is paid $15 for an hour.

(a) How many hours does he need to proofread six chapters?

(b) What is the total amount of money he will be paid for proofreading the six chapters?

Singapore Math Practice Level 3B

1.  The bar graph shows the favorite fruit of the students in Mrs. William's class. Study the bar graph carefully, and fill in each blank with the correct answer.

**Favorite Fruit of Mrs. William's Class**

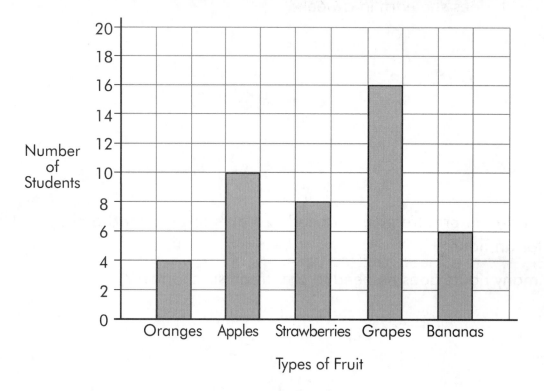

(a) _____ students like strawberries.

(b) _____ students like bananas.

(c) There are _____ more students who like grapes than apples.

(d) There are _____ fewer students who like oranges than bananas.

(e) There are _____ students in the class altogether.

**Fill in each blank to make the fractions equivalent.**

2. $\dfrac{2}{9} = \dfrac{\square}{45}$

3. $\dfrac{3}{7} = \dfrac{12}{\square}$

**Write each fraction in its simplest form.**

4. $\dfrac{8}{10} = \dfrac{\square}{\square}$

5. $\dfrac{15}{25} = \dfrac{\square}{\square}$

**Fill in each blank with the correct answer.**

6. 76 min. = _____ hr. _____ min.

7. 4 hr. 15 min. = _____ min.

**Solve each of the following problems.**

8. $\dfrac{1}{4} + \dfrac{2}{8} + \dfrac{3}{8} =$

9. $1 - \dfrac{1}{5} - \dfrac{7}{10} =$

Singapore Math Practice Level 3B

10. Circle the larger fraction.

   (a)  $\dfrac{4}{5}$  and  $\dfrac{3}{10}$

   (b)  $\dfrac{8}{9}$  and  $\dfrac{2}{3}$

11. Circle the smaller fraction.

   (a)  $\dfrac{2}{3}$  and  $\dfrac{2}{7}$

   (b)  $\dfrac{3}{8}$  and  $\dfrac{1}{4}$

12. Arrange the fractions in order. Begin with the largest.

   $\dfrac{2}{3},\ \dfrac{1}{6},\ \dfrac{3}{6}$ _____

13. Arrange the fractions in order. Begin with the smallest.

   $\dfrac{1}{3},\ \dfrac{1}{5},\ \dfrac{1}{9}$ _____

**Fill in each blank with the correct answer.**

14.

_____ to _____

15. 4 hr. 35 min. + 3 hr. 30 min. = ____ hr. ____ min.

Singapore Math Practice Level 3B

16. Consuela had just received her test scores. Her scores for the four tests are shown in the table below.

| English | Math | Science | Social Studies |
|---------|------|---------|----------------|
| 95 | 80 | 75 | 80 |

(a) Use the information above to complete the bar graph.

**Consuela's Test Scores**

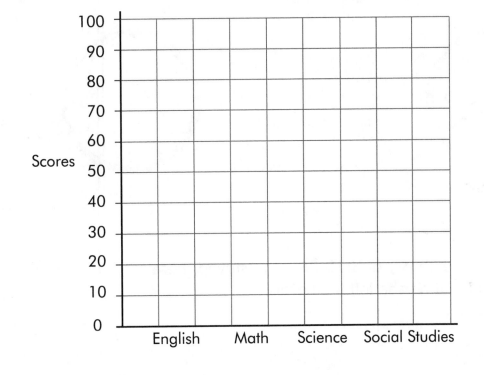

(b) Consuela scored the lowest in _____.

(c) Consuela scored _____ points more in math than in science.

(d) Consuela scored _____ points less in social studies than in English.

**Fill in each blank with the correct answer.**

17. 9 hr. 15 min. – 3 hr. 45 min. = ____ hr. ____ min.

Singapore Math Practice Level 3B

# Draw the correct time on the face of each clock.

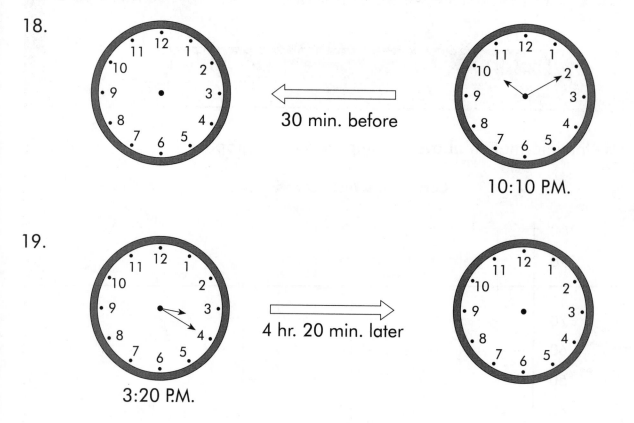

18.

30 min. before

10:10 P.M.

19.

3:20 P.M.

4 hr. 20 min. later

20. Maggie went to the library at 3:15 P.M. She stayed there for 2 hr. 25 min. Draw a timeline to find the time she left the library.

Singapore Math Practice Level 3B

# Unit 16: ANGLES

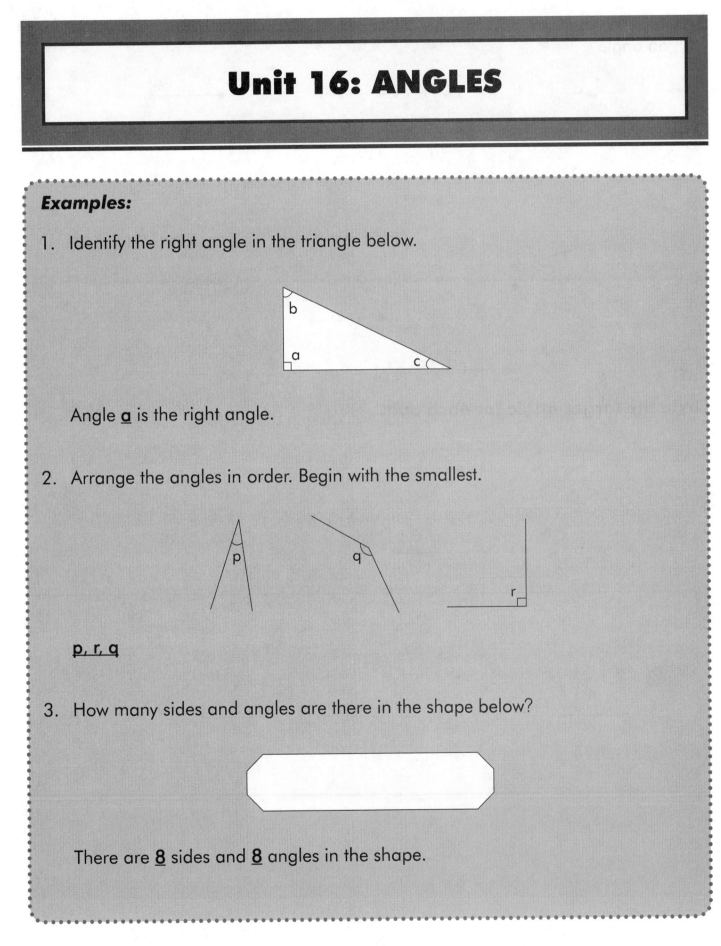

**Examples:**

1.  Identify the right angle in the triangle below.

    Angle **a** is the right angle.

2.  Arrange the angles in order. Begin with the smallest.

    **p, r, q**

3.  How many sides and angles are there in the shape below?

    There are **8** sides and **8** angles in the shape.

Singapore Math Practice Level 3B

1. Amit arranges some toothpicks as shown below. Circle the arrangements that form an angle.

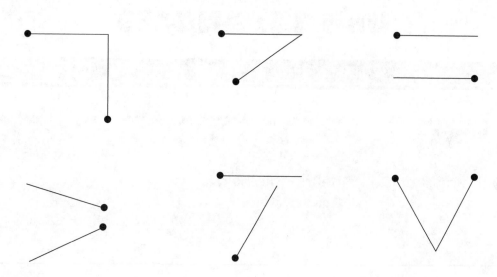

**Circle the larger angle for each pair.**

2.

3.

4.

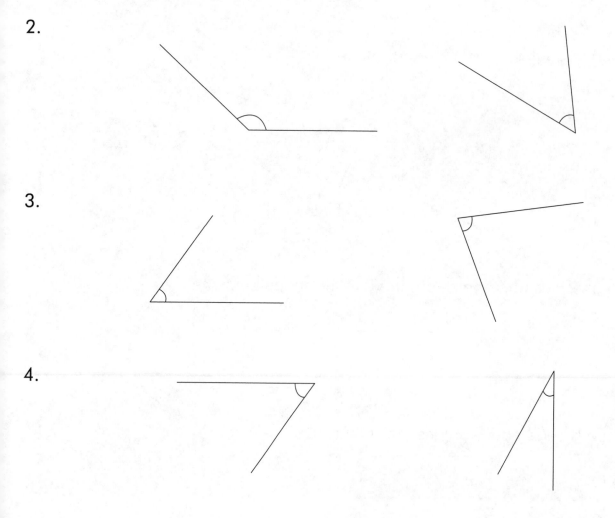

Singapore Math Practice Level 3B

5.

6.

**Circle the smaller angle for each pair.**

7.

8.

9.

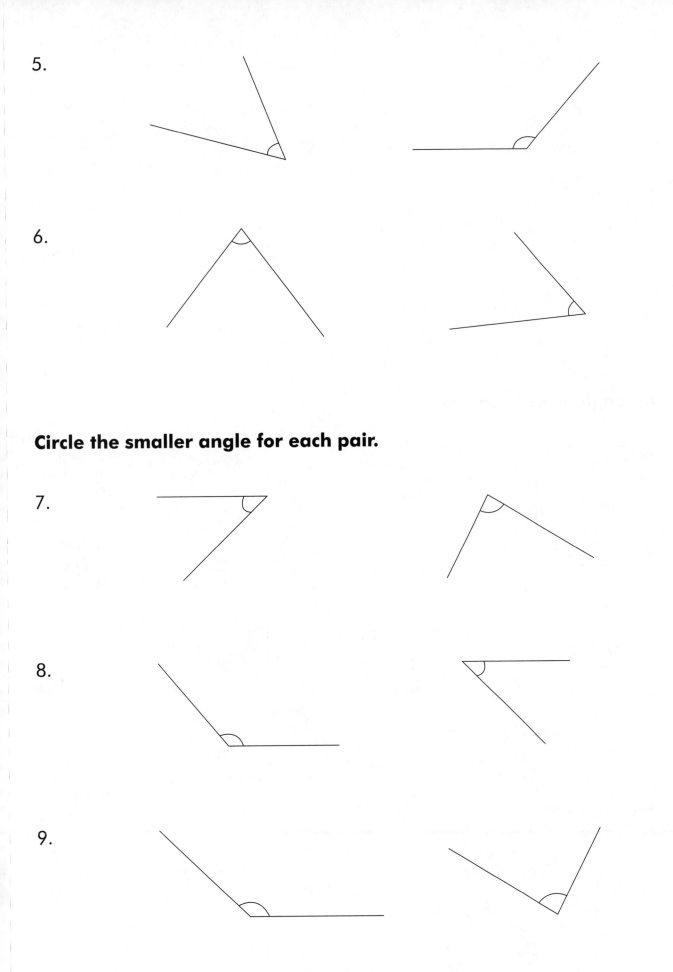

10.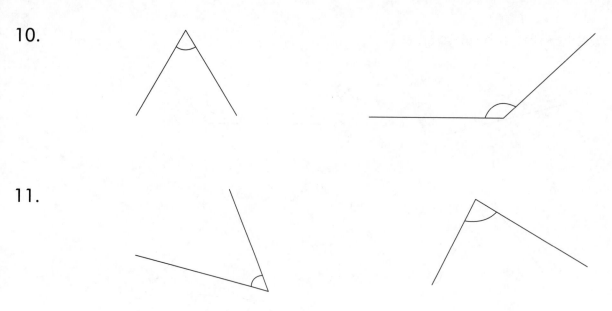

11.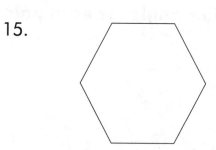

**Mark one angle in each shape.**

12.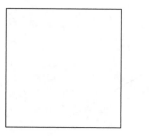

13.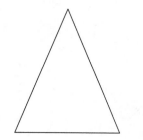

14.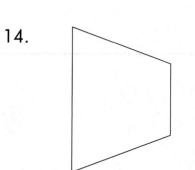

15.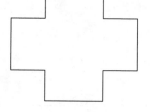

16.

# Mark one angle in each object.

17.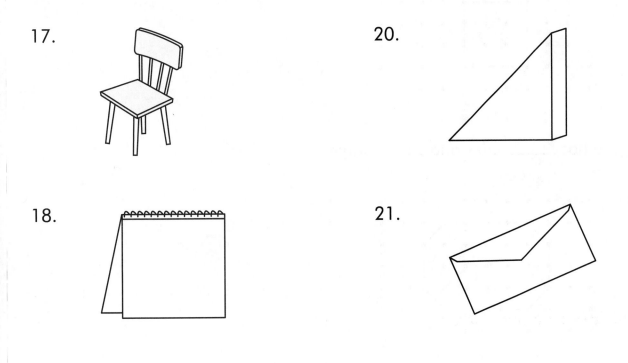

20.

18.

21.

19.

# Fill in each blank with the correct answer.

22.

This figure has _____ sides and _____ angles.

Singapore Math Practice Level 3B

23.

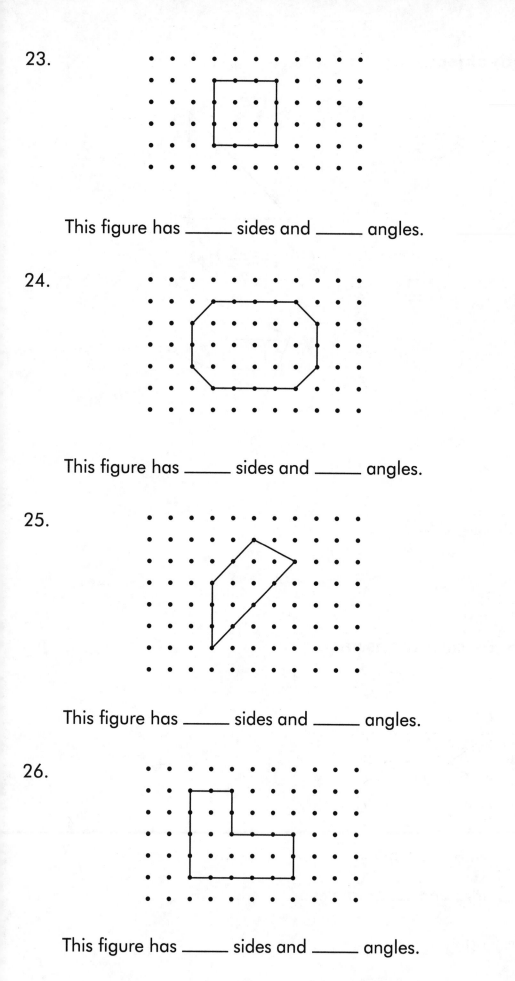

This figure has _____ sides and _____ angles.

24.

This figure has _____ sides and _____ angles.

25.

This figure has _____ sides and _____ angles.

26.

This figure has _____ sides and _____ angles.

Singapore Math Practice Level 3B

# Mark all the right angles in each figure.

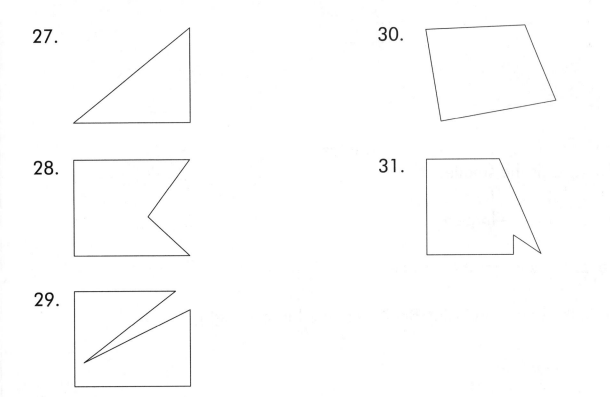

27.

28.

29.

30.

31.

32. Study the following angles carefully. Fill in each blank with the correct answer.

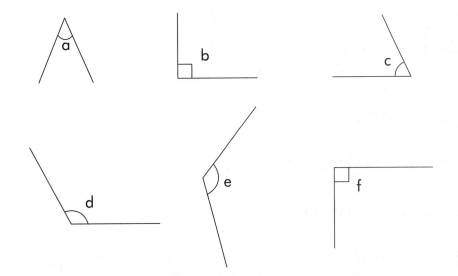

(a) Which angles are smaller than a right angle? _____

(b) Which angles are larger than a right angle? _____

(c) Which angles are right angles? _____

Singapore Math Practice Level 3B

33. Study the following angles carefully. Fill in each blank with the correct answer.

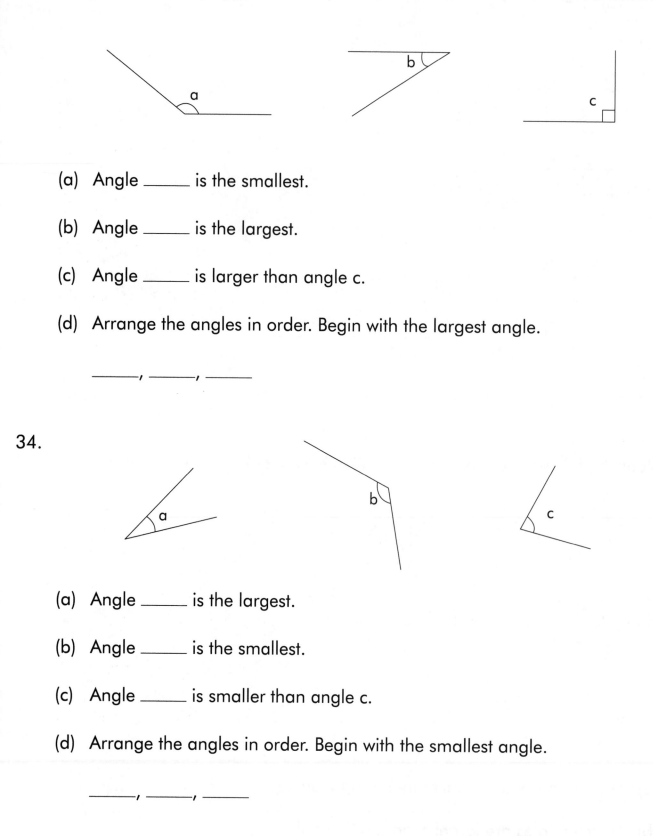

(a) Angle _____ is the smallest.

(b) Angle _____ is the largest.

(c) Angle _____ is larger than angle c.

(d) Arrange the angles in order. Begin with the largest angle.

_____, _____, _____

34.

(a) Angle _____ is the largest.

(b) Angle _____ is the smallest.

(c) Angle _____ is smaller than angle c.

(d) Arrange the angles in order. Begin with the smallest angle.

_____, _____, _____

Singapore Math Practice Level 3B

**Fill in each blank with the correct answer.**

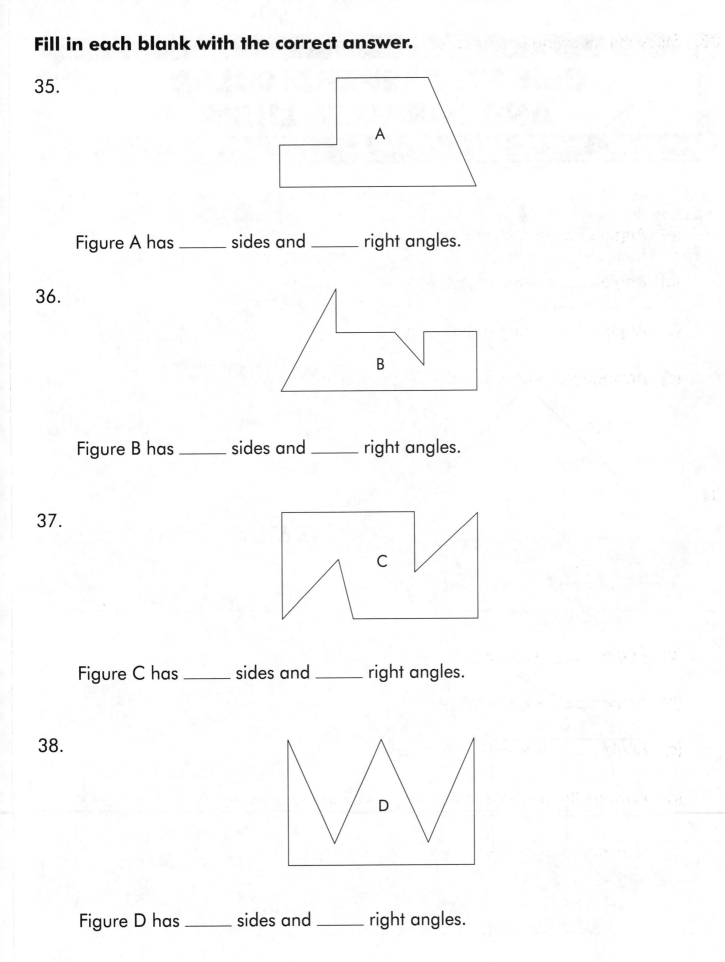

35.

Figure A has _____ sides and _____ right angles.

36.

Figure B has _____ sides and _____ right angles.

37.

Figure C has _____ sides and _____ right angles.

38.

Figure D has _____ sides and _____ right angles.

Singapore Math Practice Level 3B

# Unit 17: PERPENDICULAR AND PARALLEL LINES

**Examples:**

1. Is AB perpendicular to (⊥) CD?

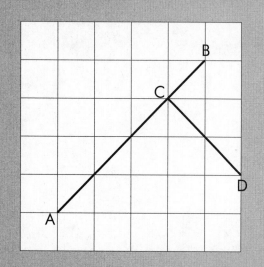

Yes, AB is perpendicular to (⊥) CD.

2. Identify all parallel lines.

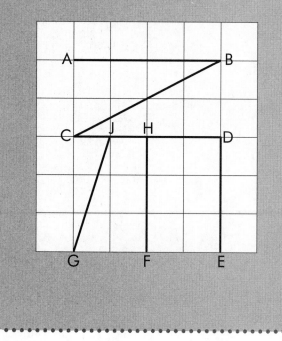

AB is parallel to (//) CD.

DE is parallel to (//) HF.

Singapore Math Practice Level 3B

**Put a check mark (✓) in the box if the pair of lines is perpendicular. Put an X if the pair of lines is not perpendicular.**

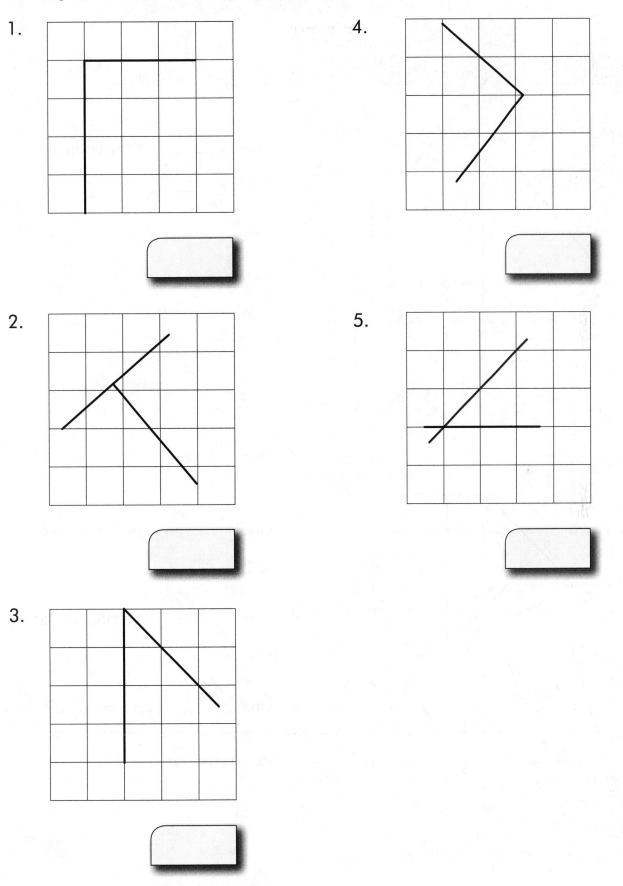

1.

2.

3.

4.

5.

Singapore Math Practice Level 3B

**Fill in each blank with the correct answer.**

6.

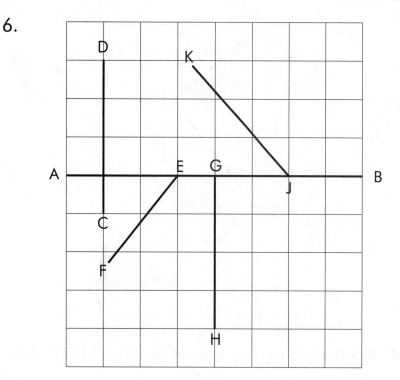

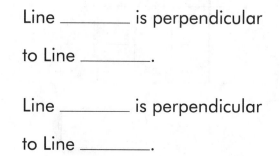

Line _____ is perpendicular

to Line _____.

Line _____ is perpendicular

to Line _____.

7.

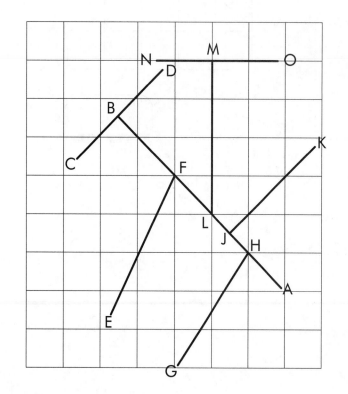

Line _____ is perpendicular

to Line _____.

Line _____ is perpendicular

to Line _____.

Line _____ is perpendicular

to Line _____.

Singapore Math Practice Level 3B

**For each figure, identify all pairs of perpendicular lines.**

8.                                                 9.

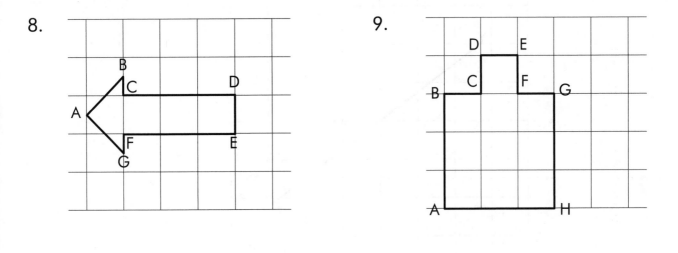

_____

**Draw 3 lines perpendicular to YZ. Each line must pass through at least two points on the grid.**

10.

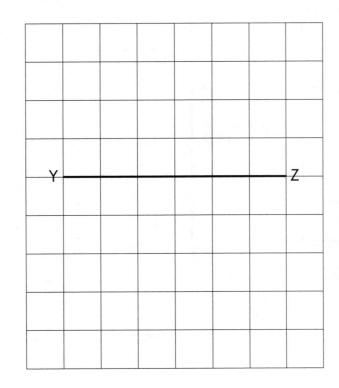

Singapore Math Practice Level 3B

11.

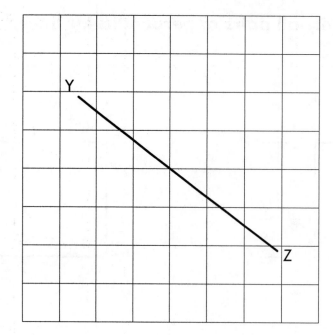

12.

Singapore Math Practice Level 3B

**Put a check mark (✓) in the box if the pair of lines is parallel. Put an X if the pair of lines is not parallel.**

13.

16.

14.

17.

15.

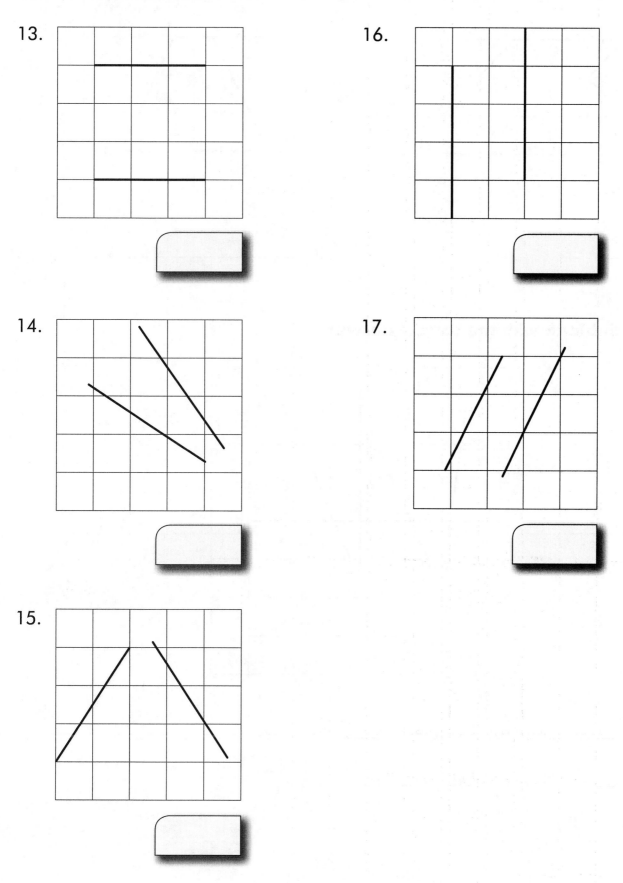

Singapore Math Practice Level 3B

**For each figure, identify the pairs of parallel lines.**

18.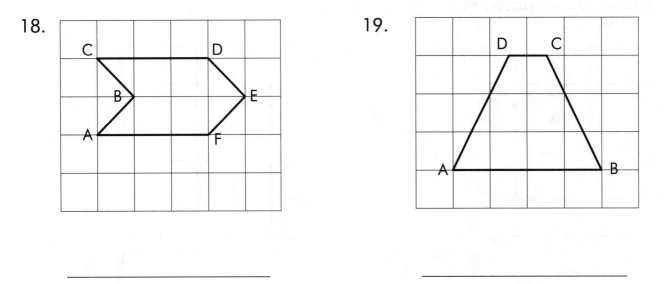

19.

_____    _____

**Fill in each blank with the correct answer.**

20.

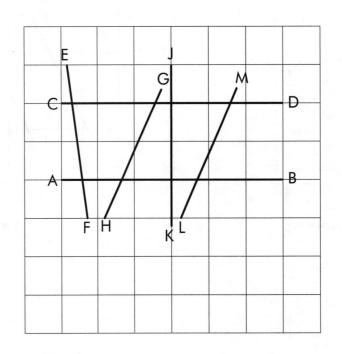

Line _____ is parallel to Line _____.

Line _____ is parallel to Line _____.

Singapore Math Practice Level 3B

**21.**

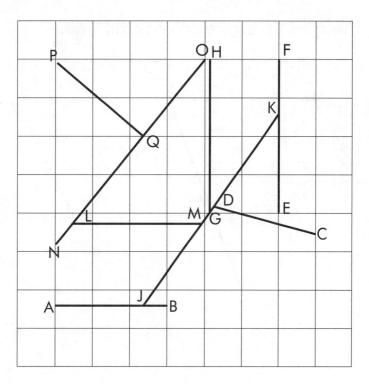

Line _____ is parallel to Line _____.

Line _____ is parallel to Line _____.

Line _____ is parallel to Line _____.

**Draw 2 lines parallel to YZ. Each line must pass through at least two points on the grid.**

**22.**

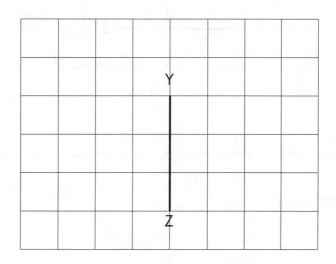

Singapore Math Practice Level 3B

**23.**

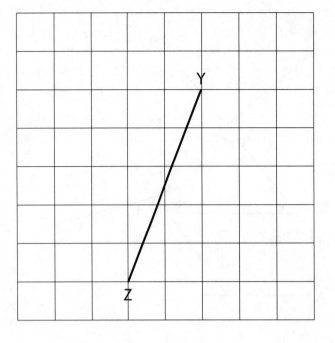

**24.**

Singapore Math Practice Level 3B

# Unit 18: AREA AND PERIMETER

**Examples:**

1. Find the area of the figure below.

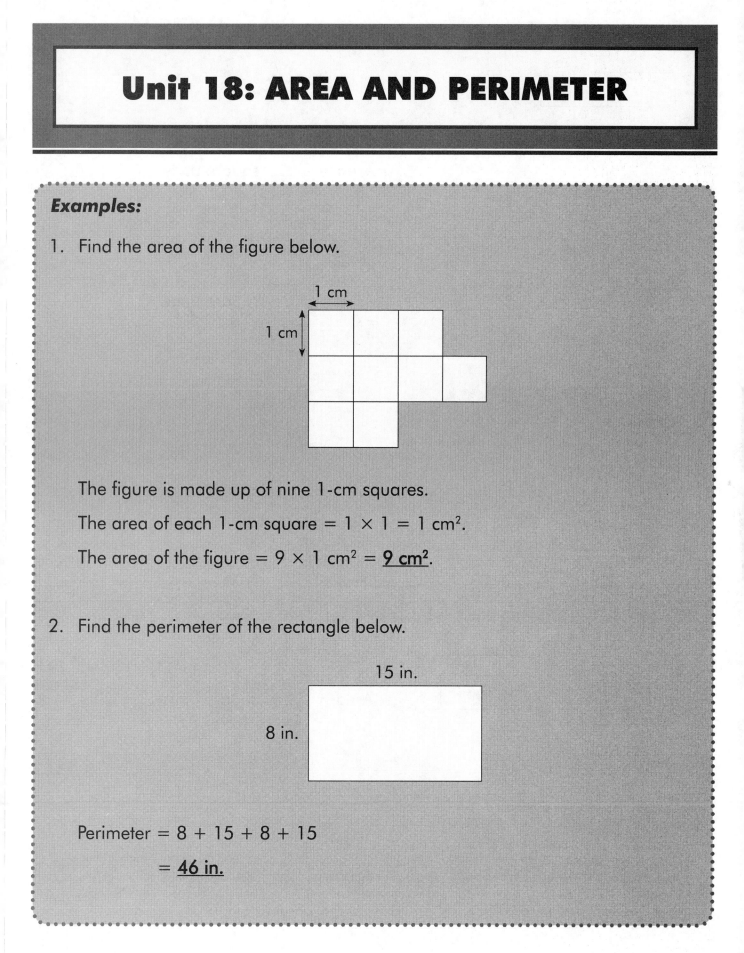

The figure is made up of nine 1-cm squares.

The area of each 1-cm square = $1 \times 1 = 1 \text{ cm}^2$.

The area of the figure = $9 \times 1 \text{ cm}^2 = \underline{\textbf{9 cm}^2}$.

2. Find the perimeter of the rectangle below.

Perimeter = $8 + 15 + 8 + 15$

= $\underline{\textbf{46 in.}}$

Singapore Math Practice Level 3B

# Find the area of each figure.

1.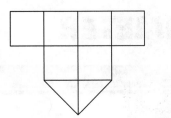

Area = _____ square units

2.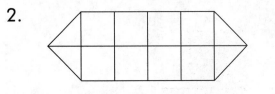

Area = _____ square units

3.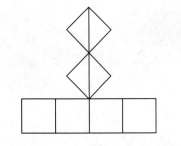

Area = _____ square units

4.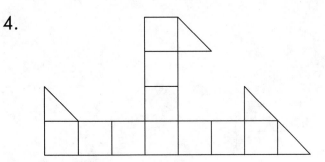

Area = _____ square units

5.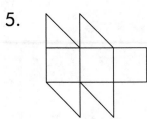

Area = _____ square units

Singapore Math Practice Level 3B

6. The area of each square is 1 cm². Find the area of the shaded figures below.

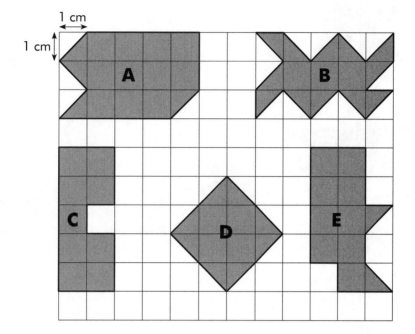

(a) The area of Figure A is _____ cm².

(b) The area of Figure B is _____ cm².

(c) The area of Figure C is _____ cm².

(d) The area of Figure D is _____ cm².

(e) The area of Figure E is _____ cm².

(f) Figures _____ and _____ have the same area.

(g) Figure _____ has the smallest area.

(h) Figure _____ has the largest area.

# Find the perimeter of each shaded figure.

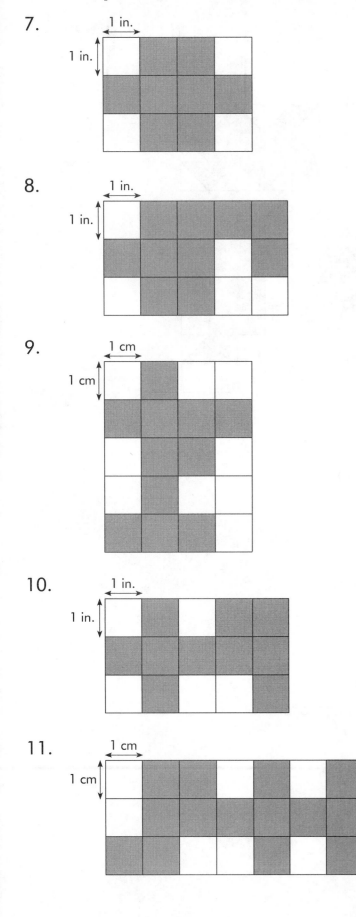

7.

1 in.

1 in.

Perimeter = _____ in.

8.

1 in.

1 in.

Perimeter = _____ in.

9.

1 cm

1 cm

Perimeter = _____ cm

10.

1 in.

1 in.

Perimeter = _____ in.

11.

1 cm

1 cm

Perimeter = _____ cm

Singapore Math Practice Level 3B

12. Study the following figures carefully. Fill in each blank with the correct answer.

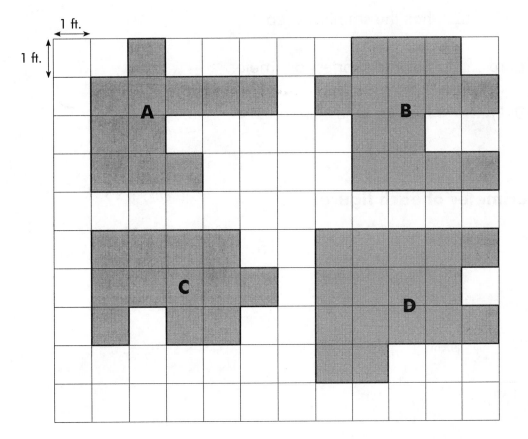

(a) The area of Figure A is _____ ft.².

(b) The area of Figure B is _____ ft.².

(c) The area of Figure C is _____ ft.².

(d) The area of Figure D is _____ ft.².

(e) The perimeter of Figure A is _____ ft.

(f) The perimeter of Figure B is _____ ft.

(g) The perimeter of Figure C is _____ ft.

(h) The perimeter of Figure D is _____ ft.

Singapore Math Practice Level 3B

(i)   Figure _____ has the largest area.

(j)   Figure _____ has the smallest area.

(k)   Figure _____ has the shortest perimeter.

(l)   Figure _____ has the longest perimeter.

## Find the perimeter of each figure.

13.

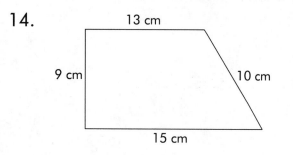

Perimeter = _____ cm

15.

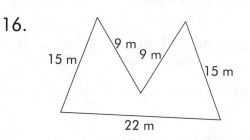

Perimeter = _____ in.

14.

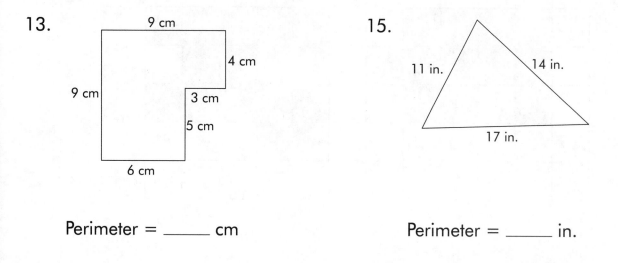

Perimeter = _____ cm

16.

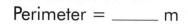

Perimeter = _____ m

Singapore Math Practice Level 3B

# Find the area and perimeter of each figure.

**17.**

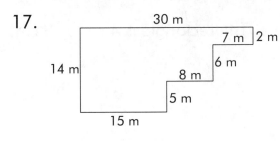

Perimeter = _____ m

**20.**

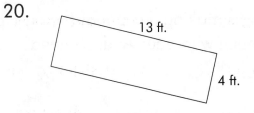

Area = _____ ft.²

Perimeter = _____ ft.

**18.**

Area = _____ in.²

Perimeter = _____ in.

**21.**

Area = _____ cm²

Perimeter = _____ cm

**19.**

Area = _____ cm²

Perimeter = _____ cm

**22.**

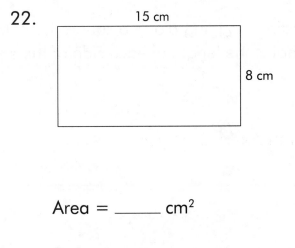

Area = _____ cm²

Perimeter = _____ cm

Singapore Math Practice Level 3B

**Solve the following story problems. Show your work in the space below.**

23. Andrew is making a rectangle using a piece of wire. The rectangle is 4 cm by 8 cm. How much wire does Andrew need?

24. Mercy sweeps the kitchen. The kitchen is 6 m by 8 m. How much floor space does Mercy sweep?

25. Justin is jogging along a square field. If he has jogged 240 yd. to complete 1 lap, what is the length of each side of the square field?

Singapore Math Practice Level 3B

# REVIEW 3

1. Mark all angles smaller than a right angle in the figure below.

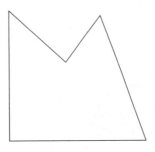

## Fill in each blank with the correct answer.

2.

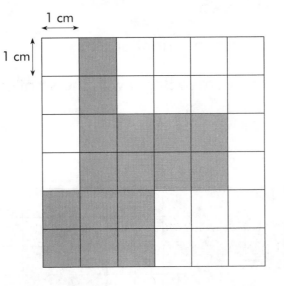

   (a) The area of the above figure is _____ cm².

   (b) The perimeter of the above figure is _____ cm.

3.

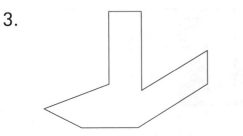

This figure has _____ sides and _____ right angles.

4.  Identify all the perpendicular lines in the figure below.

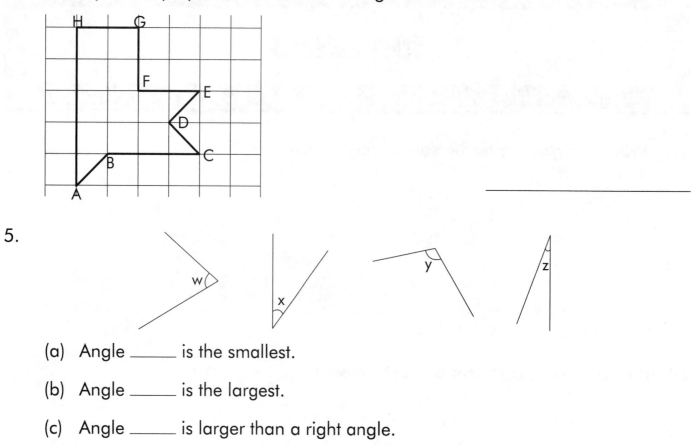

_____

5.

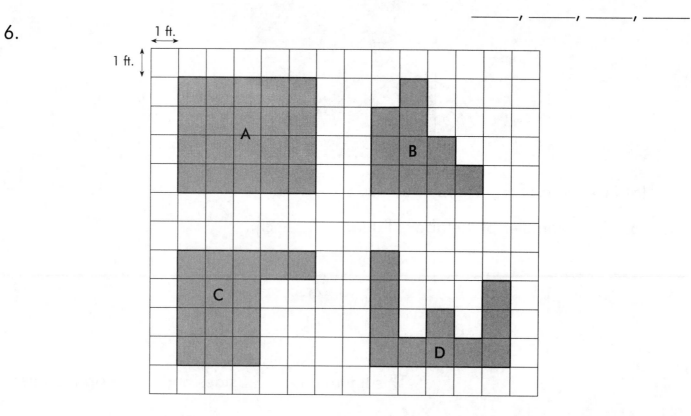

(a) Angle _____ is the smallest.

(b) Angle _____ is the largest.

(c) Angle _____ is larger than a right angle.

(d) Arrange the angles in order. Begin with the smallest angle.

_____ , _____ , _____ , _____

6.

Singapore Math Practice Level 3B

(a)  The area of Figure A is _____ ft.².

(b)  The area of Figure B is _____ ft.².

(c)  The area of Figure C is _____ ft.².

(d)  The area of Figure D is _____ ft.².

(e)  The perimeter of Figure A is _____ ft.

(f)  The perimeter of Figure B is _____ ft.

(g)  The perimeter of Figure C is _____ ft.

(h)  The perimeter of Figure D is _____ ft.

(i)  Figure _____ has the smallest area.

(j)  Figure _____ has the longest perimeter.

7.  Identify all the parallel lines in the figure below.

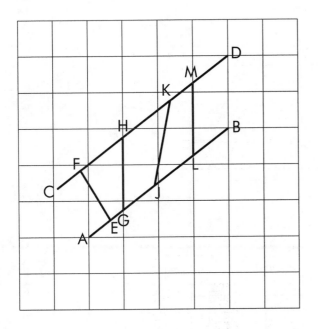

8. Find the perimeter of the figure below.

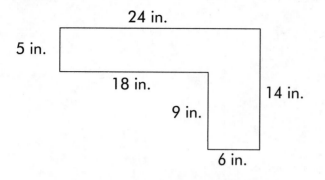

9. Identify two pairs of parallel lines in the figure below.

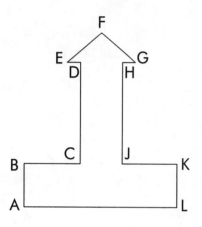

10. Draw 2 lines perpendicular to Line CD. Each line must pass through at least two points on the grid.

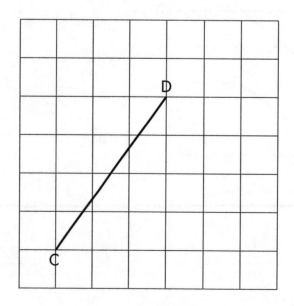

Singapore Math Practice Level 3B

11. Mark all the right angles in the figure below.

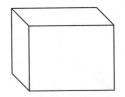

12. Find the area and perimeter of the figure below.

32 in.

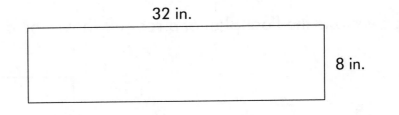

8 in.

Area = _____ in.²          Perimeter = _____ in.

13. Find the area of the square.

12 cm

_____

**Solve the following story problems. Show your work in the space below.**

14. The figure below is made up of four squares. Find the perimeter of the figure.

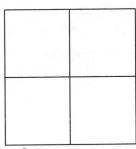

9 cm

Singapore Math Practice Level 3B

15. The width of a box is 15 in. Its length is twice its width. What is the perimeter of the box?

16. The figure below shows the floor plan of a room. What is the area of the room?

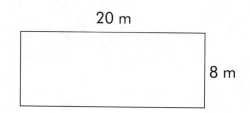

20 m

8 m

17. Emma has a piece of wrapping paper 30 in. by 15 in. She uses 80 in.² of the wrapping paper. What is the area of the remaining wrapping paper?

18. Jennifer uses half of a piece of drawing paper. The remaining drawing paper measures 14 cm by 11 cm. What is the total area of the piece of drawing paper?

19. Becky cuts a rectangle from a piece of cardboard as shown below. What is the perimeter of the remaining cardboard?

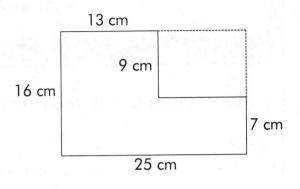

20. Nathan glued two similar rectangular stickers on a piece of paper as shown below. Find the perimeter of the two stickers.

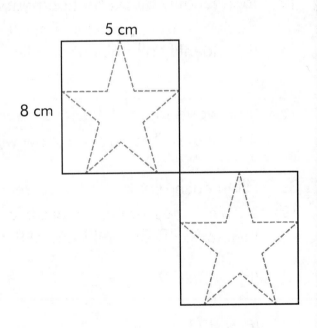

# FINAL REVIEW

**Fill in each blank with the correct answer.**

1.

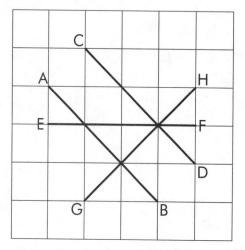

(a)   Identify all pairs of perpendicular lines.        _____

(b)   Identify all pairs of parallel lines.              _____

2.   Sam wants to watch his favorite cartoon show. It starts at 4:45 P.M. The cartoon lasts 45 minutes. The cartoon show will end at _____.

3.   Fill in each blank with the correct answer.

(a)   307 cm = _____ m _____ cm

(b)   43 kg 210 g = _____ g

(c)   80 L 10 mL = _____ mL

(d)   4 km 40 m = _____ m

Singapore Math Practice Level 3B

4. The bar graph shows the different types of products sold at a bookstore in a day.

**Types of Products Sold at a Bookstore**

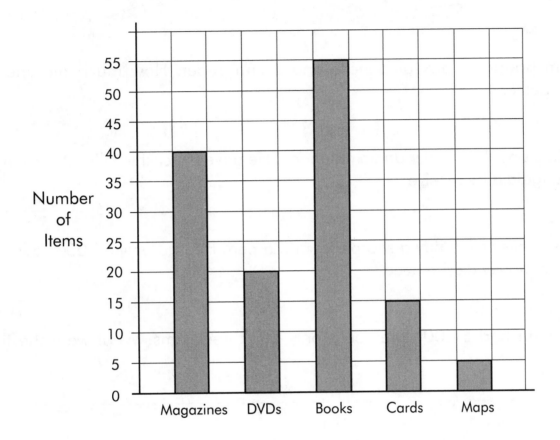

Number of Items (y-axis)

Types of food

(a) The item that sold the most was _____.

(b) _____ magazines were sold.

(c) There were _____ more books sold than cards.

(d) There were _____ fewer maps sold than DVDs.

(e) A total of _____ cards and maps were sold.

Singapore Math Practice Level 3B

5. Below are some items sold in an office supply store.

box of pencils     notebook     pen     sharpener     file folder

$2.35     $1.60     $1.35     $0.95     $2.00

(a) Pam bought a box of pencils and a sharpener. How much did she pay altogether?

_____

(b) Felipe bought a folder and a notebook. He gave the cashier $5.00. How much change did he receive?

_____

(c) Austin needed to buy a sharpener and a pen. He had only $2.00. How much more money did he need?

_____

(d) Adriana had $4.00. She could only buy three items. What were the three items?

_____

6. Fill in each box with the correct answer to make the fraction equivalent.

(a) $\dfrac{3}{7} = \dfrac{9}{\Box}$

(c) $\dfrac{8}{11} = \dfrac{32}{\Box}$

(b) $\dfrac{2}{4} = \dfrac{\Box}{16}$

(d) $\dfrac{4}{9} = \dfrac{\Box}{27}$

7. Write each fraction in its simplest form.

(a) $\dfrac{8}{12} = \dfrac{\Box}{\Box}$

(c) $\dfrac{6}{8} = \dfrac{\Box}{\Box}$

(b) $\dfrac{3}{6} = \dfrac{\Box}{\Box}$

(d) $\dfrac{4}{10} = \dfrac{\Box}{\Box}$

Singapore Math Practice Level 3B

8.  Find the area of the shaded figure.

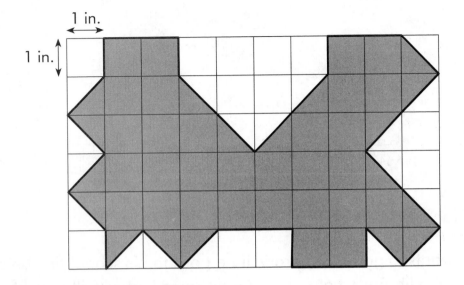

The area of the shaded figure is _____ in.².

9.  In the figure below, identify all the angles smaller than a right angle by marking them.

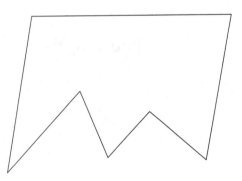

10. Arrange the fractions in order. Begin with the smallest.

$\dfrac{3}{8}$, $\dfrac{3}{4}$, $\dfrac{1}{4}$          _____ , _____ , _____

11. Study the map below and answer the questions.

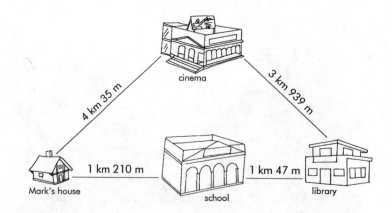

(a) How far is the cinema from Mark's house?

_____ m

(b) Mark wants to go to the library. If he goes to his school first before making his way to the library, what is the total distance that he will travel from his house?

_____ m

(c) If Mark goes to the library by passing the cinema from his house, what is the total distance that he will cover?

_____ km _____ m

(d) Which is a shorter route to the library, by the cinema or by the school?

_____

(e) How much shorter?

_____ km _____ m

**Solve the addition problems below.**

12. $360.50 + $197.85 = $_____

13. 10 m 36 cm − 2 m 77 cm = _____ m _____ cm

14. 7 km 4 m + 9 km 312 m = _____ km _____ m

15. $469.20 − $87.90 = $_____

16. 63 L 97 mL − 42 L 656 mL = _____ L _____ mL

17. 44 kg 300 g + 29 kg 695 g = _____ kg _____ g

Singapore Math Practice Level 3B

18. Fill in each blank with *kg* or *g*.

    (a)  The mass of a ruler is 15 _____.

    (b)  The mass of a dictionary is 1 _____.

19.     The time is 1:25 P.M. 30 minutes later, the time will be

    _____.

20. Find the sum of $\frac{1}{9}$ and $\frac{2}{3}$.                    _____

**Solve the following story problems. Show your work in the space below.**

21. Robert is helping to pour a concrete patio. The patio is 12 ft. long and 10 ft. wide. What is the area of the patio?

22. An elephant has a mass of 125 kg 600 g. A lion has a mass of 60 kg 700 g lighter than the elephant. What is the total mass of the two animals?

Singapore Math Practice Level 3B

23. Marley bought a sofa set and a table. The sofa set cost $3,700, and the table cost $1,900 less than the sofa set. How much did Marley pay for the furniture in all?

24. A ship leaves the port and travels 93 km 650 m to Town B. It then travels to Town C which is 6 km 770 m away from Town B. How far does the ship travel altogether?

25. Mary cooked 10 L 50 mL of chicken soup on Saturday. She cooked 8 L 960 mL more chicken soup on Sunday than on Saturday. What was the total volume of chicken soup that she had cooked on both days?

Singapore Math Practice Level 3B

# CHALLENGE QUESTIONS

**Solve the following word problems on another sheet of paper.**

1. Mike bought a backpack that cost $29.90. He gave the cashier the exact amount with 7 bills and 4 coins. What were the bills and coins he gave to the cashier?

2. A garden is located exactly halfway between Jamie's house and her school. The distance between the garden and her school is 1 km. What is the distance from Jamie's house to her school?

3. Replace the following letters with digits 1, 2, 3, and 4. The addition of AB and CD is 46. The addition of DC and BA is 64. Find the digits that represent letters A, B, C, and D.

4. Plant A is 1 m tall. Plant B is 50 cm taller than Plant A. Plant C is 5 cm shorter than Plant A. What is the total height of the tallest and the shortest plants?

5. Mr. Robinson flew from Singapore to Tokyo, Japan. The flight lasted 7 hours. Tokyo is an hour ahead of the time in Singapore. If Mr. Robinson reached Tokyo at 7 A.M. on September 14, find the time his flight left Singapore.

6. Grace dropped a string into a measuring cylinder of oil and water. $\frac{1}{4}$ of the string was immersed in oil and water. $\frac{1}{8}$ of the string was immersed in water. If 5 cm of the string was immersed in water, what was the total length of the string?

7. Ken has 3 bills. The first bill is twice the amount of money of the second one. The third bill is ten times the amount of money of the second one. The difference between the largest and the smallest amounts is $45. How much money does Ken have?

Singapore Math Practice Level 3B

8.  It is 12 hours earlier in New York than in Singapore. What will be the time in New York when the clock strikes twelve midnight on Christmas Day in Singapore?

9.  Simon's father ate $\frac{1}{2}$ of a pizza. Simon ate $\frac{1}{2}$ of what was left. Simon's mother ate $\frac{1}{2}$ of what was left after Simon had taken his pieces. The remaining 2 pieces of pizza were eaten by Simon's brother. How many pieces of pizza were there at first?

10. Mrs. David bought groceries. She gave the cashier $25. She received the change in 3 bills in two different denominations. One of the bills was 5 times the amount of money of the other bills. The change was between $5 and $10. How much were the groceries?

11. A bean plant grows 1 inch every three days. How tall will the bean plant grow after 30 days?

12. Study the numbers carefully. Find the missing number.

| 118 | 159 | 277 |
|-----|-----|-----|
| 269 | ?   | 623 |
| 387 | 513 | 900 |

Singapore Math Practice Level 3B

# SOLUTIONS
## Singapore Math Practice Level 3B

**Unit 10: Money**

1. **8.35**
$5 + $3 = $8
$8 + 35¢ = $8.35

2. **51.20**
$43 + $8 = $51
$51 + 20¢ = $51.20

3. **104.75**
$14 + $90 = $104
$104 + 75¢ = $104.75

4. **98.90**
$30 + $68 = $98
$98 + 90¢ = $98.90

5. **9.60**
5¢ + 55¢ = 60¢
$9 + 60¢ = $9.60

6. **24.90**
$24 + 90¢ = $24.90

7. **70.80**
$70 + 80¢ = $70.80

8. **89.20**
20¢ + $6.80 = $7
$82.20 + $7 = $89.20

9. **55.85**
$53 + $2 = $55
60¢ + 25¢ = 85¢
$55 + 85¢ = $55.85

10. **45.30**
20¢ + $1.80 = $2
$43.30 + $2 = $45.30

11. **18.20, 1.00**
**19.20, 30**
**18.90**

12. **26.90, 1.00**
**27.90, 20**
**27.70**

13. **72.50, 1.00**
**73.50, 10**
**73.40**

14. **59.60, 1.00**
**60.60, 20**
**60.40**

15. **76.40, 1.00**
**77.40, 30**
**77.10**

16.
$23.50
+ $13.20
**$36.70**

17.
$ 86.75
+ $ 37.45
**$124.20**

18.
$515.55
+ $  79.25
**$594.80**

19.
$4.35
+ $0.90
**$5.25**

20.
$73.20
+ $18.00
**$91.20**

21.
$125.80
+ $214.40
**$340.20**

22.
$217.00
+ $142.85
**$359.85**

23.
$  56.20
+ $  64.15
**$120.35**

24.
$49.70
+ $28.50
**$78.20**

25.
$67.90
+ $17.70
**$85.60**

26. **34.40**
$39 − $5 = $34
$34 + 40¢ = $34.40

27. **74.55**
$78 − $4 = $74
$74 + 55¢ = $74.55

28. **36.10**
70¢ − 60¢ = 10¢
$36 + 10¢ = $36.10

29. **82.55**
75¢ − 20¢ = 55¢
$82 + 55¢ = $82.55

30. **48.15**
60¢ − 45¢ = 15¢
$48 + 15¢ = $48.15

31. **99.15**
50¢ − 35¢ = 15¢
$99 + 15¢ = $99.15

32. **83.20**
30¢ − 10¢ = 20¢
$87 − $4 = $83
$83 + 20¢ = $83.20

33. **66.20**
55¢ − 35¢ = 20¢
$69 − $3 = $66
$66 + 20¢ = $66.20

34. **91.30**
60¢ − 30¢ = 30¢
$92 − $1 = $91
$91 + 30¢ = $91.30

35. **51.30**
80¢ − 50¢ = 30¢
$58 − $7 = $51
$51 + 30¢ = $51.30

36. **67.40, 1.00**
**66.40, 20**
**66.60**

37. **46.20, 1.00**
**45.20, 30**
**45.50**

38. **28.30, 1.00**
**27.30, 10**
**27.40**

39. **70.60, 1.00**
**69.60, 20**
**69.80**

40. **45.20, 1.00**
**44.20, 10**
**44.30**

41.
$7.80
− $3.50
**$4.30**

42.
$50.00
− $ 5.60
**$44.40**

43.
$280.50
− $  66.60
**$213.90**

44.
$23.10
− $ 2.30
**$20.80**

45.
$758.70
− $329.40
**$429.30**

46.
$143.05
− $ 21.80
**$121.25**

47.
$955.60
− $  89.45
**$866.15**

48.
$49.25
− $ 5.60
**$43.65**

49.
$10.00
− $ 3.45
**$ 6.55**

50.
$659.20
− $ 92.25
**$566.95**

51. (a) **8.80**
$3.20 + $5.60 = $8.80

(b) **12.95**
$5.60 + $7.35 = $12.95

(c) **kite and a box of crayons**
$1.15 + $3.20 = $4.35

(d) **7.40**
$11.45 + $1.15 = $12.60
$20 − $12.60 = $7.40

(e) **3.25**
$7.35 − $4.10 = $3.25

52.
| $1.10 | $3.50 |
|-------|-------|
| ? |

$1.10 + $3.50 = $4.60
Ashley pays **$4.60** altogether.

53.
| $75.35 | ? |
|--------|---|
| $100 |

**117**

$100 – $75.35 = $24.65
She would receive **$24.65** in change.

54.

$500 + $200 = $700
$700 + $500 = $1,200
His parents received **$1,200** altogether.

55.

$75.70 + $125 = $200.70
$200.70 + $360.00 = $560.70
She spends **$560.70** altogether every month.

56.

$750 – $200 = $550
The chairs cost **$550**.

57.

$500 + $350 = $850
$1,000 – $850 = $150
Beth had to save **$150** in March.

58.

4 × $10.00 = $40.00
$40.00 – $34.90 = $5.10
She should receive **$5.10** in change.

59. (a)

$19.65 + $43.60 = $63.25
Aaron had **$63.25** at first.

(b)

$80.35 + $19.65 = $100.00
$100.00 – $63.25 = $36.75
Andy had **$36.75** more than Aaron.

## Unit 11: Length, Mass, and Volume

1. **3, 23**
   300 cm + 23 cm = 3 m 23 cm
2. **7, 10**
   700 cm + 10 cm = 7 m 10 cm
3. **8, 5**
   800 cm + 5 cm = 8 m 5 cm
4. **10, 0**
   1,000 cm = 10 m
5. **15, 25**
   1,500 cm + 25 cm = 15 m 25 cm
6. **5, 21**
   500 cm + 21 cm = 5 m 21 cm
7. **6, 6**
   600 cm + 6 cm = 6 m 6 cm

8. **21, 56**
   2,100 cm + 56 cm = 21 m 56 cm
9. **0, 43**
10. **23, 36**
    2,300 cm + 36 cm = 23 m 36 cm
11. **434**
    400 cm + 34 cm = 434 cm
12. **110**
    100 cm + 10 cm = 110 cm
13. **1,005**
    1,000 cm + 5 cm = 1,005 cm
14. **656**
    600 cm + 56 cm = 656 cm
15. **2,000**
    20 × 100 = 2,000 cm
16. **808**
    800 cm + 8 cm = 808 cm
17. **1,530**
    1,500 cm + 30 cm = 1,530 cm
18. **789**
    700 cm + 89 cm = 789 cm
19. **3,140**
    3,100 cm + 40 cm = 3,140 cm
20. **945**
    900 cm + 45 cm = 945 cm
21. **1, 456**
    1,000 m + 456 m = 1 km 456 m
22. **6, 830**
    6,000 m + 830 m = 6 km 830 m
23. **1, 0**
    1,000 m = 1 km
24. **6, 592**
    6,000 m + 592 m = 6 km 592 m
25. **9, 225**
    9,000 m + 225 m = 9 km 225 m
26. **4, 50**
    4,000 m + 50 m = 4 km 50 m
27. **8, 3**
    8,000 m + 3 m = 8 km 3 m
28. **2, 6**
    2,000 m + 6 m = 2 km 6 m
29. **3, 100**
    3,000 m + 100 m = 3 km 100 m
30. **7, 707**
    7,000 m + 707 m = 7 km 707 m
31. **3,850**
    3,000 m + 850 m = 3,850 m
32. **1,070**
    1,000 m + 70 m = 1,070 m
33. **5,000**
    5 × 1,000 = 5,000 m
34. **9,220**
    9,000 m + 220 m = 9,220 m
35. **12,500**
    12,000 m + 500 m = 12,500 m
36. **27,003**
    27,000 m + 3 m = 27,003 m
37. **9,090**
    9,000 m + 90 m = 9,090 m
38. **20,100**
    20,000 m + 100 m = 20,100 m
39. **2,300**
    2,000 m + 300 m = 2,300 m

Singapore Math Practice Level 3B

40. **1,309**
    1,000 m + 309 m = 1,309 m
41. (a) **2,700, 2, 700**    (c) **1,500, 1, 500**
    (b) **2,350, 2, 350**    (d) **1,070, 1, 70**
42. **km**
43. **cm**
44. **cm**
45. **m**
46. **1,000**
    1 × 1,000 = 1,000 g
47. **1,238**
    1,000 g + 238 g = 1,238 g
48. **3,300**
    3,000 g + 300 g = 3,300 g
49. **9,569**
    9,000 g + 569 g = 9,569 g
50. **5,955**
    5,000 g + 955 g = 5,955 g
51. **7,067**
    7,000 g + 67 g = 7,067 g
52. **10,760**
    10,000 g + 760 g = 10,760 g
53. **4,008**
    4,000 g + 8 g = 4,008 g
54. **8,642**
    8,000 g + 642 g = 8,642 g
55. **2,484**
    2,000 g + 484 g = 2,484 g
56. **1, 369**
    1,000 g + 369 g = 1 kg 369 g
57. **4, 820**
    4,000 g + 820 g = 4 kg 820 g
58. **12, 790**
    12,000 g + 790 g = 12 kg 790 g
59. **6, 606**
    6,000 g + 606 g = 6 kg 606 g
60. **10, 1**
    10,000 g + 1 g = 10 kg 1 g
61. **3, 33**
    3000 g + 33 g = 3 kg 33 g
62. **5, 115**
    5,000 g + 115 g = 5 kg 115 g
63. **8, 780**
    8,000 g + 780 g = 8 kg 780 g
64. **2, 200**
    2,000 g + 200 g = 2 kg 200 g
65. **9, 90**
    9,000 g + 90 g = 9 kg 90 g
66. **600**
67. **1,800**
68. **2,500**
69. **660**
70. **2,600**
71. **150**
72. **g**
73. **kg**
74. **kg**
75. **g**
76. **300**
77. **750**
    500 mL + 250 mL = 750 mL
78. **1, 300**
    1 L + 300 mL = 1 L 300 mL

79. **2, 70**
    1 L + 1 L + 70 mL = 2 L 70 mL
80. **350**
    100 mL + 100 mL + 150 mL = 350 mL
81. **1, 590**
    1 L + 500 mL + 90 mL = 1 L 590 mL
82. **1,000**
    1 × 1,000 = 1,000 mL
83. **4,368**
    4,000 mL + 368 mL = 4,368 mL
84. **10,010**
    10,000 mL + 10 mL = 10,010 mL
85. **8,818**
    8,000 mL + 818 mL = 8,818 mL
86. **12,200**
    12,000 mL + 200 mL = 12,200 mL
87. **3,008**
    3,000 mL + 8 mL = 3,008 mL
88. **8,096**
    8,000 mL + 96 mL = 8,096 mL
89. **7,478**
    7,000 mL + 478 mL = 7,478 mL
90. **9,009**
    9,000 mL + 9 mL = 9,009 mL
91. **11,110**
    11,000 mL + 110 mL = 11,110 mL
92. **4, 352**
    4,000 mL + 352 mL = 4 L 352 mL
93. **9, 909**
    9,000 mL + 909 mL = 9 L 909 mL
94. **3, 100**
    3,000 mL + 100 mL = 3 L 100 mL
95. **8, 702**
    8,000 mL + 702 mL = 8 L 702 mL
96. **2, 0**
    2,000 mL + 0 mL = 2 L 0 mL
97. **5, 15**
    5,000 mL + 15 mL = 5 L 15 mL
98. **7, 7**
    7,000 mL + 7 mL = 7 L 7 mL
99. **6, 60**
    6,000 mL + 60 mL = 6 L 60 mL
100. **10, 1**
    10,000 mL + 1 mL = 10 L 1 mL
101. **1, 100**
    1,000 mL + 100 mL = 1 L 100 mL
102. **mL**
103. **L**
104. **mL**
105. **L**

## Unit 12: Problem Solving (Length, Mass, and Volume)

1. 
$$\begin{array}{r} \overset{2}{\cancel{3}}\overset{11}{\cancel{2}}\overset{15}{\cancel{5}} \\ -\phantom{0}88 \\ \hline 237 \end{array}$$
    325 – 88 = 237
    The length of the wooden plank is **237 cm**.

2. 
$$\begin{array}{r} 168 \\ 5\overline{)840} \\ \underline{5}\phantom{00} \\ 34\phantom{0} \\ \underline{30}\phantom{0} \\ 40 \\ \underline{40} \\ 0 \end{array}$$
    840 ÷ 5 = 168
    The length of each piece of ribbon is **168 cm**.

**3.**

| 38 kg | 37 kg |
|---|---|

?

38 + 37 = 75
Their total mass is **75 kg**.

$$\begin{array}{r} \overset{1}{3}\,8 \\ +\ 3\,7 \\ \hline 7\,5 \end{array}$$

**4.**

| ? | 900 g |
|---|---|

3,000 g

3,000 − 900 = 2100
2,100 g = 2,000 g + 100 g = 2 kg 100 g
She used **2 kg 100 g** of flour.

$$\begin{array}{r} \overset{2}{\cancel{3}},\overset{10}{\cancel{0}}\,0\,0 \\ -\ \ \ 9\,0\,0 \\ \hline 2,1\,0\,0 \end{array}$$

**5.**

| 7,900 mL | ? |
|---|---|

10,360 mL

10,360 − 7,900 = 2,460
She adds **2,460 mL** of milk.

$$\begin{array}{r} \overset{0}{1}\overset{9}{0},\overset{13}{3}\,6\,0 \\ -\ 7,9\,0\,0 \\ \hline 2,4\,6\,0 \end{array}$$

**6.**

| ? | 18 L |
|---|---|

40 L

40 − 18 = 22
She has used up **22 L** of gasoline.

$$\begin{array}{r} \overset{3}{\cancel{4}}\overset{10}{\cancel{0}} \\ -\ 1\,8 \\ \hline 2\,2 \end{array}$$

**7.**

| ? | ? | ? |
|---|---|---|

1,800 g

1,800 ÷ 3 = 600
The mass of each box of crackers was **600 g**.

**8.**

| 550 mL | 550 mL | 550 mL | 550 mL | 550 mL | 550 mL | 550 mL | 550 mL | 550 mL | 550 mL | 550 mL | 550 mL |
|---|---|---|---|---|---|---|---|---|---|---|---|

?

550 × 12 = 6,600
6,600 mL = 6,000 mL + 600 mL
= 6 L 600 mL
She bought **6 L 600 mL** of orange juice.

$$\begin{array}{r} \overset{1}{5}\,5\,0 \\ \times\ \ \ 1\,2 \\ \hline 4,1\,0\,0 \\ 5\,5\,0\ \ \\ \hline 6,6\,0\,0 \end{array}$$

**9.**

272 cm

| | | ? |
|---|---|---|

555 cm

555 − 272 = 283
283 cm = 200 cm + 83 cm = 2 m 83 cm
The length of the third stick is **2 m 83 cm**.

$$\begin{array}{r} \overset{4}{\cancel{5}}\overset{15}{\cancel{5}}\,5 \\ -\ 2\,7\,2 \\ \hline 2\,8\,3 \end{array}$$

**10.**

table | 3,960 g |
chair | 2,700 g | ?

3,960 − 2,700 = 1,260
The table is **1,260 g** heavier than the chair.

$$\begin{array}{r} 3,9\,6\,0 \\ -\ 2,7\,0\,0 \\ \hline 1,2\,6\,0 \end{array}$$

**11.** 8 + 6 + 8 + 6 = 28
The fence will be **28 m** long.

8 m
6 m

**12.**

Basir | 4,870 g |
Andy | ? | 3,560 g | ?

4,870 − 3,560 = 1,310
Andy's bag of groceries is 1,310 g.
4,870 + 1,310 = 6,180
6,180 g = 6,000 g + 180 g = 6 kg 180 g
Andy and Basir's bags of groceries are **6 kg 180 g**.

$$\begin{array}{r} 4,8\,7\,0 \\ -\ 3,5\,6\,0 \\ \hline 1,3\,1\,0 \end{array}$$

$$\begin{array}{r} \overset{1}{4},8\,7\,0 \\ +\ 1,3\,1\,0 \\ \hline 6,1\,8\,0 \end{array}$$

**13.**

| 30,960 g | 10,040 g |
|---|---|

?

30,960 + 10,040 = 41,000

$$\begin{array}{r} \overset{1}{3}0,\overset{1}{9}\,6\,0 \\ +\ 1\,0,0\,4\,0 \\ \hline 4\,1,0\,0\,0 \end{array}$$

41,000 g = 41 kg
It sold **41 kg** of fish on both days.

**14.**

Sam | 8,300 mL |
Evan | ? | 6,970 mL | ?

8,300 − 6,970 = 1,330
Evan bought 1,330 mL of paint.
8,300 + 1,330 = 9,630
They bought **9,630 mL** of paint altogether.

$$\begin{array}{r} \overset{7}{\cancel{8}},\overset{12}{\cancel{3}}\overset{10}{\cancel{0}}\,0 \\ -\ 6,9\,7\,0 \\ \hline 1,3\,3\,0 \end{array}$$

$$\begin{array}{r} 8,3\,0\,0 \\ +\ 1,3\,3\,0 \\ \hline 9,6\,3\,0 \end{array}$$

**15.**

Kelly | 125 g | ?
Sister | | | |

125 × 4 = 500
Her sister used **500 g** more flour than Kelly.

$$\begin{array}{r} \overset{1}{1}\overset{2}{2}\,5 \\ \times\ \ \ \ 4 \\ \hline 5\,0\,0 \end{array}$$

**16.**

A | 135 cm |
B | | | | ?

135 × 4 = 540
The total height of both trees is **540 cm**.

$$\begin{array}{r} \overset{1}{1}\overset{2}{3}\,5 \\ \times\ \ \ \ 4 \\ \hline 5\,4\,0 \end{array}$$

**17.** Andre: 15 m × 3 m = 45 m²
Tim: 12 m × 4 m = 48 m²
(a) **Tim** has to paint more wall space.
(b) 48 − 45 = 3
He has to paint **3 m²** more wall space.

**18.**

?

| 1 km 400 m | 800 m | 1 km 10 m |
|---|---|---|

1 km 400 m + 800 m + 1 km 10 m = 3 km 210 m
Margaret walked a total distance of **3 km 210 m**.

**19.**

Jake | 6,500 mL | 2,765 mL
Brother | ? | ?

6,500 + 2,765 = 9,265
His brother uses 9,265 mL of water.
9,265 + 6,500 = 15,765
15,765 mL = 15,000 mL + 765 mL
= 15 L 765 mL
Both of them use **15 L 765 mL** of water.

$$\begin{array}{r} \overset{1}{6},5\,0\,0 \\ +\ 2,7\,6\,5 \\ \hline 9,2\,6\,5 \end{array}$$

$$\begin{array}{r} 9,2\,6\,5 \\ +\ 6,5\,0\,0 \\ \hline 1\,5,7\,6\,5 \end{array}$$

**20.**

| 420 mL | 420 mL | 420 mL | 420 mL | 420 mL | 420 mL | 420 mL | 420 mL |
|---|---|---|---|---|---|---|---|

?

(a) 420 × 8 = 3,360
The total volume of 8 glasses of milk was **3,360 mL**.

$$\begin{array}{r} \overset{1}{4}\,2\,0 \\ \times\ \ \ \ 8 \\ \hline 3,3\,6\,0 \end{array}$$

(b) 3,360 + 250 = 3,610
3,610 mL = 3,000 mL + 610 mL
= 3 L 610 mL
There was **3 L 610 mL** of milk in all.

$$\begin{array}{r} \overset{1}{3},3\,6\,0 \\ +\ \ \ 2\,5\,0 \\ \hline 3,6\,1\,0 \end{array}$$

**21.**

| 2 L | | 2 L |
|---|---|---|

14 L

(a) 14 ÷ 2 = 7
He could fill **7** pots of coffee.
(b) 7 − 2 = 5
**5** pots of coffee were used.

---

**Review 1**

1. (a) **4, 15**
415 cm = 400 cm + 15 cm = 4 m 15 cm
(b) **8, 30**
830 cm = 800 cm + 30 cm = 8 m 30 cm

**120**

2. (a) **6, 269**
   6,269 m = 6,000 m + 269 m = 6 km 269 m
   (b) **5, 500**
   5,500 m = 5,000 m + 500 m = 5 km 500 m

3. (a) **7, 670**
   7,670 g = 7,000 g + 670 g = 7 kg 670 g
   (b) **4, 8**
   4,008 g = 4,000 g + 8 g = 4 kg 8 g

4. (a) **4, 835**
   4,835 mL = 4,000 mL + 835 mL = 4 L 835 mL
   (b) **6, 505**
   6,505 mL = 6,000 mL + 505 mL = 6 L 505 mL

5. (a) **6,975**
   6,000 m + 975 m = 6,975 m
   (b) **8,008**
   8,000 m + 8 m = 8,008 m

6. (a) **905**
   900 cm + 5 cm = 905 cm
   (b) **1,000**
   10 × 100 = 1,000 cm

7. (a) **2,002**
   2,000 mL + 2 mL = 2,002 mL
   (b) **5,275**
   5,000 mL + 275 mL = 5,275 mL

8. (a) **2,636**
   2,000 g + 636 g = 2,636 g
   (b) **5,030**
   5,000 g + 30 g = 5,030 g

9. **2,000**
   2 kg = 2,000 g

10. 1 L + 500 mL + 70 mL = 1 L 570 mL = 1,000 mL + 570 mL
    = **1,570** mL

11. (a) **3.20**
    $1.50 + $1.70 = $3.20
    (b) **3.40**
    2 × $0.80 = $1.60
    $5.00 − $1.60 = $ 3.40
    (c) **40.55**
    4 × $10 = $40
    $40 + $0.55 = $40.55

12. (a) **850**
    (b) **1,400**
    1 km 400 m = 1,000 m + 400 m = 1,400 m
    (c) **1,175**
    1 km 175 m = 1,000 m + 175 m = 1,175 m

13.
| $1,200 | | |
|---|---|---|
| $500 | $375 | ? |

   $500 + $375 = $875
   $1,200 − $875 = $325
   Ken saves **$325**.

```
  $ 5 0 0
+ $ 3 7 5
  $ 8 7 5

   0 11 9 10
$ 1, 2 0 0
−  $  8 7 5
$     3 2 5
```

14.
| 8 km 120 m | 8 km 120 m |
|---|---|

   ?

   8 km 120 m + 8 km 120 m = 16 km 240 m
   Benjamin jogs **16 km 240 m** daily.

15.
   Alex | $410 |
   Sam | $75 |
   John | $160 |
   ?

   $410 − $75 = $335
   $335 + $160 = $495
   John spends **$495**.

```
   3 10 10
 $ 4 1 0
−  $  7 5
 $ 3 3 5

 $ 3 3 5
+$ 1 6 0
 $ 4 9 5
```

16.
   cement | 4 kg 360 g |
   sand | 2 kg 500 g | ?

   (a) 4 kg 360 g − 2 kg 500 g = 1 kg 860 g
   He mixes **1 kg 860 g** more cement.
   (b) 4 kg 360 g + 2 kg 500 g = 6 kg 860 g
   The total mass of the mixture is
   **6 kg 860 g**.

```
   3  13
 4, 3 6 0
− 2, 5 0 0
  1, 8 6 0

 4, 3 6 0
+ 2, 5 0 0
 6, 8 6 0
```

17.
   5 m 70 cm
   | 2 m 25 cm | ? |

   (a) 5 m 70 cm − 2 m 25 cm = 3 m 45 cm
   **Pole B** is longer.
   (b) 3 m 45 cm − 2 m 25 cm = 1 m 20 cm
   Pole B is **120 cm** longer than Pole A.

```
   6 10
 5 7 0
− 2 2 5
  3 4 5

  3 4 5
− 2 2 5
  1 2 0
```

18.
   | 250 mL | 250 mL | 250 mL | 250 mL |
   ?

   250 × 4 = 1,000
   1,000 mL = 1 L
   The total volume of the four cartons of milk is **1 L**.

```
    2
   2 5 0
 ×     4
 1, 0 0 0
```

19.
   | $3.60 | $3.55 | ? |
   $10.00

   $3.60 + $3.55 = $7.15
   $10.00 − $7.15 = $2.85
   The oranges cost **$2.85**.

```
 $ 3 . 6 0
+$ 3 . 5 5
 $ 7 . 1 5

   0  9   9 10
$ 1 0 . 0 0
−  $  7 . 1 5
 $   2 . 8 5
```

20.
   | ? | ? | ? | ? | ? | ? |
   3 L 250 mL + 1,670 mL

   3,250 + 1,670 = 4,920
   4,920 ÷ 6 = 820
   There was **820 mL** of orange juice
   in each container.

```
    1
 3, 2 5 0
+ 1, 6 7 0
 4, 9 2 0
```

```
        8 2 0
 6 ) 4, 9 2 0
     4 8
        1 2
        1 2
         0
         0
         0
```

## Unit 13: Bar Graphs

1.
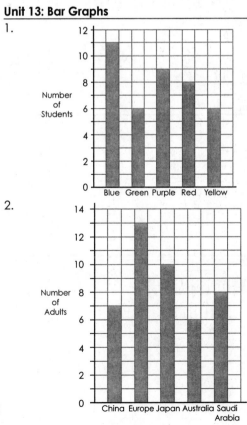

2.

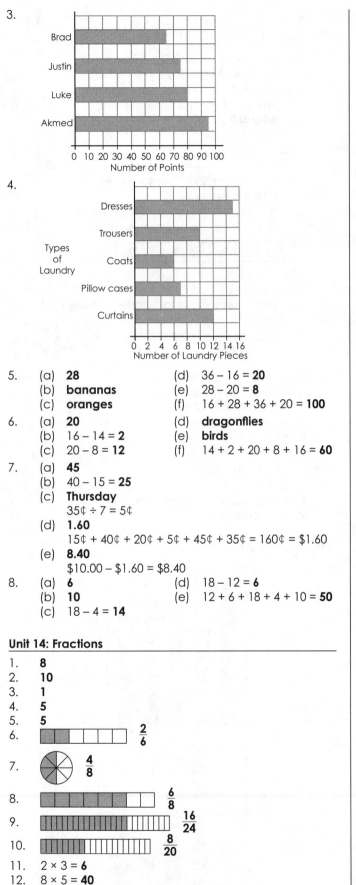

3.

Bar graph — Number of Points: Brad, Justin, Luke, Akmed (0 10 20 30 40 50 60 70 80 90 100)

4.

Bar graph — Types of Laundry: Dresses, Trousers, Coats, Pillow cases, Curtains (0 2 4 6 8 10 12 14 16) Number of Laundry Pieces

5. (a) **28**     (d) 36 − 16 = **20**
   (b) **bananas**   (e) 28 − 20 = **8**
   (c) **oranges**   (f) 16 + 28 + 36 + 20 = **100**

6. (a) **20**     (d) **dragonflies**
   (b) 16 − 14 = **2**   (e) **birds**
   (c) 20 − 8 = **12**   (f) 14 + 2 + 20 + 8 + 16 = **60**

7. (a) **45**
   (b) 40 − 15 = **25**
   (c) **Thursday**
      35¢ ÷ 7 = 5¢
   (d) **1.60**
      15¢ + 40¢ + 20¢ + 5¢ + 45¢ + 35¢ = 160¢ = $1.60
   (e) **8.40**
      $10.00 − $1.60 = $8.40

8. (a) **6**     (d) 18 − 12 = **6**
   (b) **10**    (e) 12 + 6 + 18 + 4 + 10 = **50**
   (c) 18 − 4 = **14**

## Unit 14: Fractions

1. **8**
2. **10**
3. **1**
4. **5**
5. **5**
6. $\frac{2}{6}$
7. $\frac{4}{8}$
8. $\frac{6}{8}$
9. $\frac{16}{24}$
10. $\frac{8}{20}$
11. 2 × 3 = **6**
12. 8 × 5 = **40**
13. 3 × 4 = **12**
14. 10 × 8 = **80**

15. 9 × 7 = **63**
16. 4 × 4 = **16**
17. 7 × 3 = **21**
18. 2 × 6 = **12**
19. 11 × 7 = **77**
20. 3 × 6 = **18**
21. **2, 15, 20, 25**
    1 × 2 = 2
    5 × 3 = 15
    5 × 4 = 20
    5 × 5 = 25
22. **6, 9, 32, 40**
    3 × 2 = 6
    3 × 3 = 9
    8 × 4 = 32
    8 × 5 = 40
23. **10, 6, 20, 25**
    5 × 2 = 10
    2 × 3 = 6
    5 × 4 = 20
    5 × 5 = 25
24. **8, 3, 16, 20**
    4 × 2 = 8
    1 × 3 = 3
    4 × 4 = 16
    4 × 5 = 20
25. **2, 3, 28, 35**
    1 × 2 = 2
    1 × 3 = 3
    7 × 4 = 28
    7 × 5 = 35
26. $\frac{7 \div 7}{21 \div 7} = \frac{1}{3}$
27. $\frac{3 \div 3}{9 \div 3} = \frac{1}{3}$
28. $\frac{8 \div 8}{16 \div 8} = \frac{1}{2}$
29. $\frac{36 \div 9}{45 \div 9} = \frac{4}{5}$
30. $\frac{35 \div 7}{42 \div 7} = \frac{5}{6}$
31. $\frac{9 \div 9}{63 \div 9} = \frac{1}{7}$
32. $\frac{44 \div 22}{66 \div 22} = \frac{2}{3}$
33. $\frac{64 \div 8}{72 \div 8} = \frac{8}{9}$
34. $\frac{12 \div 6}{18 \div 6} = \frac{2}{3}$
35. $\frac{9 \div 3}{24 \div 3} = \frac{3}{8}$
36. $\frac{3}{6}, \frac{2}{6}$
37. $\frac{4}{10}, \frac{5}{10}$
38. $\frac{4}{8}, \frac{5}{8}$
39. $\frac{7}{12}, \frac{6}{12}$
40. $\frac{3}{4}, \frac{2}{4}$
41. $\frac{1}{6}$
42. $\frac{2}{9}$

43. $\frac{3}{9}$
44. $\frac{5}{11}$
45. $\frac{7}{12}$
46. $\frac{2}{3}$
    $\frac{2 \times 4}{3 \times 4} = \frac{8}{12}$
47. $\frac{2}{5}$
    $\frac{3 \times 5}{8 \times 5} = \frac{15}{40}$
    $\frac{2 \times 8}{5 \times 8} = \frac{16}{40}$
48. $\frac{4}{6}$
    $\frac{2 \times 2}{8 \times 2} = \frac{4}{16}$
49. $\frac{2}{7}$
    $\frac{1 \times 2}{9 \times 2} = \frac{2}{18}$
50. $\frac{3}{11}$
    $\frac{1 \times 3}{4 \times 3} = \frac{3}{12}$
51. $\frac{8}{9}, \frac{5}{9}, \frac{3}{9}$
52. $\frac{3}{4}, \frac{4}{6}, \frac{2}{8}$
    $\frac{4 \times 4}{6 \times 4} = \frac{16}{24}$
    $\frac{2 \times 3}{8 \times 3} = \frac{6}{24}$
    $\frac{3 \times 6}{4 \times 6} = \frac{18}{24}$
53. $\frac{3}{4}, \frac{7}{12}, \frac{1}{6}$
    $\frac{3 \times 3}{4 \times 3} = \frac{9}{12}$
    $\frac{1 \times 2}{6 \times 2} = \frac{2}{12}$
54. $\frac{8}{9}, \frac{2}{5}, \frac{4}{15}$
    $\frac{2 \times 4}{5 \times 4} = \frac{8}{20}$
    $\frac{4 \div 2}{15 \div 2} = \frac{8}{30}$
55. $\frac{6}{7}, \frac{6}{9}, \frac{6}{12}$
56. $\frac{2}{5}, \frac{2}{4}, \frac{2}{3}$
57. $\frac{1}{4}, \frac{3}{8}, \frac{4}{6}$
    $\frac{3 \times 3}{8 \times 3} = \frac{9}{24}$
    $\frac{4 \times 4}{6 \times 4} = \frac{16}{24}$
    $\frac{1 \times 6}{4 \times 6} = \frac{6}{24}$
58. $\frac{1}{5}, \frac{3}{6}, \frac{6}{10}$
    $\frac{3 \times 2}{6 \times 2} = \frac{6}{12}$
    $\frac{1 \times 6}{5 \times 6} = \frac{6}{30}$

Singapore Math Practice Level 3B

59. $\dfrac{11}{20}, \dfrac{12}{20}, \dfrac{18}{20}$

60. $\dfrac{4}{7}, \dfrac{2}{3}, \dfrac{5}{6}$

$\dfrac{4^{\times 5}}{7^{\times 5}} = \dfrac{20}{35}$

$\dfrac{5^{\times 4}}{6^{\times 4}} = \dfrac{20}{24}$

$\dfrac{2^{\times 10}}{3^{\times 10}} = \dfrac{20}{30}$

61. $\dfrac{2^{\times 3}}{3^{\times 3}} + \dfrac{1}{9} = \dfrac{6}{9} + \dfrac{1}{9} = \dfrac{7}{9}$

62. $\dfrac{1}{4} + \dfrac{1^{\times 2}}{2^{\times 2}} = \dfrac{1}{4} + \dfrac{2}{4} = \dfrac{3}{4}$

63. $\dfrac{5}{12} + \dfrac{1^{\times 2}}{6^{\times 2}} = \dfrac{5}{12} + \dfrac{2}{12} = \dfrac{7}{12}$

64. $\dfrac{2^{\times 2}}{5^{\times 2}} + \dfrac{3}{10} = \dfrac{4}{10} + \dfrac{3}{10} = \dfrac{7}{10}$

65. $\dfrac{3}{8} + \dfrac{1^{\times 2}}{4^{\times 2}} = \dfrac{3}{8} + \dfrac{2}{8} = \dfrac{5}{8}$

66. $\dfrac{1^{\times 5}}{2^{\times 5}} - \dfrac{1^{\times 2}}{5^{\times 2}} = \dfrac{5}{10} - \dfrac{2}{10} = \dfrac{3}{10}$

67. $\dfrac{4^{\times 2}}{5^{\times 2}} - \dfrac{7}{10} = \dfrac{8}{10} - \dfrac{7}{10} = \dfrac{1}{10}$

68. $\dfrac{7}{8} - \dfrac{3^{\times 2}}{4^{\times 2}} = \dfrac{7}{8} - \dfrac{6}{8} = \dfrac{1}{8}$

69. $\dfrac{5^{\times 2}}{6^{\times 2}} - \dfrac{5}{12} = \dfrac{10}{12} - \dfrac{5}{12} = \dfrac{5}{12}$

70. $\dfrac{4}{9} - \dfrac{1^{\times 3}}{3^{\times 3}} = \dfrac{4}{9} - \dfrac{3}{9} = \dfrac{1}{9}$

71. $\dfrac{1}{9} + \dfrac{1^{\times 3}}{3^{\times 3}} + \dfrac{4}{9} = \dfrac{1}{9} + \dfrac{3}{9} + \dfrac{4}{9} = \dfrac{8}{9}$

72. $\dfrac{1^{\times 2}}{4^{\times 2}} + \dfrac{3}{8} + \dfrac{1}{8} = \dfrac{2}{8} + \dfrac{3}{8} + \dfrac{1}{8} = \dfrac{6}{8}$

73. $1 - \dfrac{7}{12} - \dfrac{1^{\times 2}}{6^{\times 2}} = \dfrac{12}{12} - \dfrac{7}{12} - \dfrac{2}{12} = \dfrac{3}{12}$

74. $1 - \dfrac{1^{\times 3}}{3^{\times 3}} - \dfrac{5}{9} = \dfrac{9}{9} - \dfrac{3}{9} - \dfrac{5}{9} = \dfrac{1}{9}$

75. $\dfrac{3}{10} + \dfrac{1^{\times 5}}{2^{\times 5}} + \dfrac{1}{10} = \dfrac{3}{10} + \dfrac{5}{10} + \dfrac{1}{10} = \dfrac{9}{10}$

76. $\dfrac{2}{6} + \dfrac{1^{\times 2}}{3^{\times 2}} + \dfrac{1}{6} = \dfrac{2}{6} + \dfrac{2}{6} + \dfrac{1}{6} = \dfrac{5}{6}$

77. $1 - \dfrac{3}{8} - \dfrac{1^{\times 4}}{2^{\times 4}} = \dfrac{8}{8} - \dfrac{3}{8} - \dfrac{4}{8} = \dfrac{1}{8}$

78. $1 - \dfrac{3^{\times 2}}{5^{\times 2}} - \dfrac{1}{10} = \dfrac{10}{10} - \dfrac{6}{10} - \dfrac{1}{10} = \dfrac{3}{10}$

## Unit 15: Time

1. **1:20**, 20 minutes after 1
2. **5:50**, 10 minutes to 6
3. **10:15**, 15 minutes after 10
4. **3:05**, 5 minutes after 3
5. **6:55**, 5 minutes to 7
6. **9:30**, 30 minutes after 9
7. **7:40**, 20 minutes to 8
8. **25**
9. **19**
10. **4**
11. **7**
12. **5**
13. **22**
14. **6**
15. **10**

16. 3 × 60 min. = **180** min.
17. 60 min. + 20 min. = **80** min.
18. 4 × 60 min. = 240 min.
    240 min. + 5 min. = **245** min.
19. 8 × 60 min. = 480 min.
    480 min. + 15 min. = **495** min.
20. 6 × 60 min. = 360 min.
    360 min. + 30 min. = **390** min.
21. 420 min. ÷ 60 min. = **7** hr.
22. 300 min. ÷ 60 min. = **5** hr.
23. 600 min. ÷ 60 min. = **10** hr.
24. 240 min. ÷ 60 min. = **4** hr.
25. 540 min. ÷ 60 min. = **9** hr.
26. 75 min. = 60 min. + 15 min. = **1** hr. **15** min.
27. 515 min. = 480 min. + 35 min. = **8** hr. **35** min.
28. 455 min. = 420 min. + 35 min. = **7** hr. **35** min.
29. 190 min. = 180 min. + 10 min. = **3** hr. **10** min.
30. 430 min. = 420 min. + 10 min. = **7** hr. **10** min.
31. **5, 50**
    5 min. + 45 min. = 50 min.
    3 hr. + 2 hr. = 5 hr.
32. **10, 55**
    17 min. + 38 min. = 55 min.
    7 hr. + 3 hr. = 10 hr.
33. **3, 58**
    19 min. + 39 min. = 58 min.
    2 hr. + 1 hr. = 3 hr.
34. **8, 9**
    13 min. + 56 min. = 69 min. = 1 hr. 9 min.
    5 hr. + 2 hr. + 1 hr. 9 min. = 8 hr. 9 min.
35. **11, 18**
    28 min. + 50 min. = 78 min. = 1 hr. 18 min.
    6 hr. + 4 hr. + 1 hr. 18 min. = 11 hr. 18 min.
36. **10, 20**
    35 min. + 45 min. = 80 min. = 1 hr. 20 min.
    8 hr. + 1 hr. + 1 hr. 20 min. = 10 hr. 20 min.
37. **2, 20**
    50 min. – 30 min. = 20 min.
    4 hr. – 2 hr. = 2 hr.
38. **3, 10**
    35 min. – 25 min. = 10 min.
    10 hr. – 7 hr. = 3 hr.
39. **5, 25**
    30 min. – 5 min. = 25 min.
    6 hr. – 1 hr. = 5 hr.
40. **4, 45**
    8 hr. 25 min. = 7 hr. 60 min. + 25 min. = 7 hr. 85 min.
    85 min. – 40 min. = 45 min.
    7 hr. – 3 hr. = 4 hr.
41. **3, 30**
    5 hr. 15 min. = 4 hr. 60 min. + 15 min. = 4 hr. 75 min.
    75 min. – 45 min. = 30 min.
    4 hr. – 1 hr. = 3 hr.
42. **5, 30**
    10 hr. 20 min. = 9 hr. 60 min + 20 min. = 9 hr. 80 min.
    80 min. – 50 min. = 30 min.
    9 hr. – 4 hr. = 5 hr.
43. **30**

    |← 30 min. →|
    4:20 P.M.          4:50 P.M.
44. **2, 15**

    |← 1 hr. →|← 1 hr. →|← 15 min. →|
    2:30 P.M.   3:30 P.M.   4:30 P.M.  4:45 P.M.

45. **3, 15**

| 1 hr. | 1 hr. | 1 hr. | 15 min. |

10:25 A.M. 11:25 A.M. 12:25 P.M. 1:25 P.M. 1:40 P.M.

46. **3, 55**

| 1 hr. | 1 hr. | 1 hr. | 20 min. | 35 min. |

11:40 A.M. 12:40 P.M. 1:40 P.M. 2:40 P.M. 3:00 P.M. 3:35 P.M.

47. **3, 45**

| 1 hr. | 1 hr. | 1 hr. | 45 min. |

7:10 P.M. 8:10 P.M. 9:10 P.M. 10:10 P.M. 10:55 P.M.

48. **8**

| 1 hr. | 1 hr. | 1 hr. | 1 hr. | 1 hr. | 1 hr. | 1 hr. | 1 hr. |

11:30 A.M. 12:30 P.M. 1:30 P.M. 2:30 P.M. 3:30 P.M. 4:30 P.M. 5:30 P.M. 6:30 P.M. 7:30 P.M.

49. **4, 40**

| 1 hr. | 1 hr. | 1 hr. | 1 hr. | 40 min. |

1:15 P.M. 2:15 P.M. 3:15 P.M. 4:15 P.M. 5:15 P.M. 5:55 P.M.

50. **7:20 A.M.**

51. **12:10 A.M.**

52. **3:10 A.M.**

53. **4:15 P.M.**

54. **12:30 P.M.**

55.

| 1 hr. | 20 min. |

5:30 P.M. 6:30 P.M. 6:50 P.M.

The movie ended at **6:50 P.M.**

56.

| 1 hr. | 1 hr. | 1 hr. | 1 hr. | 40 min. |

10:15 A.M. 11:15 A.M. 12:15 P.M. 1:15 P.M. 2:15 P.M. 2:55 P.M.

He stayed at his friend's house for **4 hr. 40 min.**

57.

| 55 mins. |

6:05 P.M. 7 P.M.

She must leave her house at **6:05 P.M.**

58. $3 + 2 + 3 + 4 + 2 + 5 = 19$ hr.
$19 \times \$125 = \$2,375$
Matt earns **\$2,375** in a week.

59. (a)

| 8 | 8 | 8 | 8 | 8 |

?

$5 \times 8 = 40$
The total number of hours she works in a week is **40 hr.**

(b) $40 \times \$9 = \$360$
She earns **\$360** in a week.

60. (a)

| 2 | 2 | 2 | 2 | 2 | 2 |

?

$6 \times 2 = 12$
He needs **12 hr.** to proofread a series of six chapters.

(b) $12 \times \$15 = \$180$
The total amount of money he will be paid for proofreading the six chapters is **\$180.**

## Review 2

1. (a) **8**
   (b) **6**
   (c) $16 - 10 = $ **6**
   (d) $6 - 4 = $ **2**
   (e) $4 + 10 + 8 + 16 + 6 = $ **44**

2. $\dfrac{2 \times 5}{9 \times 5} = \dfrac{\mathbf{10}}{\mathbf{45}}$

3. $\dfrac{3 \times 4}{7 \times 4} = \dfrac{12}{\mathbf{28}}$

4. $\dfrac{8 \div 2}{10 \div 2} = \dfrac{\mathbf{4}}{\mathbf{5}}$

5. $\dfrac{15 \div 5}{25 \div 5} = \dfrac{\mathbf{3}}{\mathbf{5}}$

6. 76 min. = 60 min. + 16 min. = **1** hr. **16** min.

7. $4 \times 60$ min. = 240 min.
240 min. + 15 min. = **255** min.

8. $\dfrac{1 \times 2}{4 \times 2} + \dfrac{2}{8} + \dfrac{3}{8} = \dfrac{2}{8} + \dfrac{2}{8} + \dfrac{3}{8} = \dfrac{\mathbf{7}}{\mathbf{8}}$

9. $1 - \dfrac{1 \times 2}{5 \times 2} - \dfrac{7}{10} = \dfrac{10}{10} - \dfrac{2}{10} - \dfrac{7}{10} = \dfrac{\mathbf{1}}{\mathbf{10}}$

10. (a) $\dfrac{\mathbf{4}}{\mathbf{5}}$
    $\dfrac{4 \times 2}{5 \times 2} = \dfrac{8}{10}$

    (b) $\dfrac{\mathbf{8}}{\mathbf{9}}$
    $\dfrac{2 \times 3}{3 \times 3} = \dfrac{6}{9}$

11. (a) $\dfrac{\mathbf{2}}{\mathbf{7}}$

    (b) $\dfrac{\mathbf{1}}{\mathbf{4}}$
    $\dfrac{1 \times 2}{4 \times 2} = \dfrac{2}{8}$

12. $\dfrac{\mathbf{2}}{\mathbf{3}}, \dfrac{\mathbf{3}}{\mathbf{6}}, \dfrac{\mathbf{1}}{\mathbf{6}}$
    $\dfrac{2 \times 2}{3 \times 2} = \dfrac{4}{6}$

13. $\dfrac{\mathbf{1}}{\mathbf{9}}, \dfrac{\mathbf{1}}{\mathbf{5}}, \dfrac{\mathbf{1}}{\mathbf{3}}$

14. **20 minutes, 7**

15. **8, 5**
    35 min. + 30 min. = 65 min. = 1 hr. 5 min.
    4 hr. + 3 hr. + 1 hr. 5 min. = 8 hr. 5 min.

16. (a)

(b) **science**
    (c) $80 - 75 = $ **5**
    (d) $95 - 80 = $ **15**

17. **5, 30**
    9 hr. 15 min. = 8 hr. 60 min. + 15 min.
    $\phantom{9 hr. 15 min. }= 8$ hr. 75 min.
    75 min. − 45 min. = 30 min.
    8 hr. − 3 hr. = 5 hr.

18.

19.

20.

| 1 hr. | 1 hr. | 25 min. |

3:15 P.M. 4:15 P.M. 5:15 P.M. 5:40 P.M.

She left the library at **5:40 P.M.**

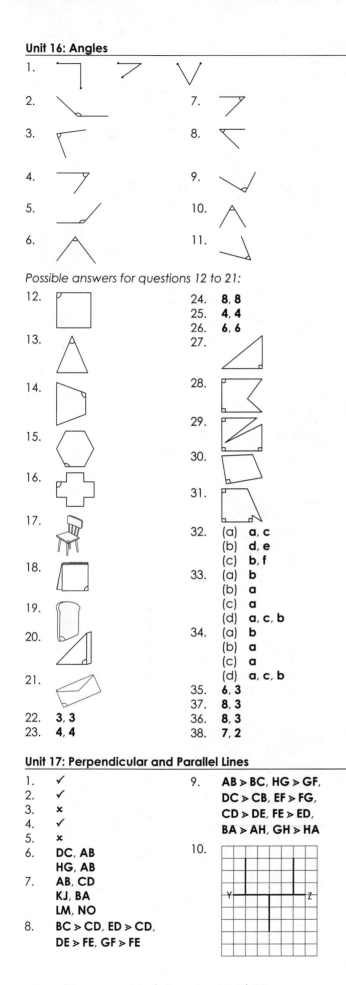

## Unit 16: Angles

1.
2.
3.
4.
5.
6.
7.
8.
9.
10.
11.

*Possible answers for questions 12 to 21:*

12.
13.
14.
15.
16.
17.
18.
19.
20.
21.
22. **3, 3**
23. **4, 4**

24. **8, 8**
25. **4, 4**
26. **6, 6**
27.
28.
29.
30.
31.
32. (a) **a, c**
    (b) **d, e**
    (c) **b, f**
33. (a) **b**
    (b) **a**
    (c) **a**
    (d) **a, c, b**
34. (a) **b**
    (b) **a**
    (c) **a**
    (d) **a, c, b**
35. **6, 3**
37. **8, 3**
36. **8, 3**
38. **7, 2**

## Unit 17: Perpendicular and Parallel Lines

1. ✓
2. ✓
3. ✗
4. ✓
5. ✗
6. **DC, AB**
   **HG, AB**
7. **AB, CD**
   **KJ, BA**
   **LM, NO**
8. **BC ⊥ CD, ED ⊥ CD,**
   **DE ⊥ FE, GF ⊥ FE**

9. **AB ⊥ BC, HG ⊥ GF,**
   **DC ⊥ CB, EF ⊥ FG,**
   **CD ⊥ DE, FE ⊥ ED,**
   **BA ⊥ AH, GH ⊥ HA**

10.

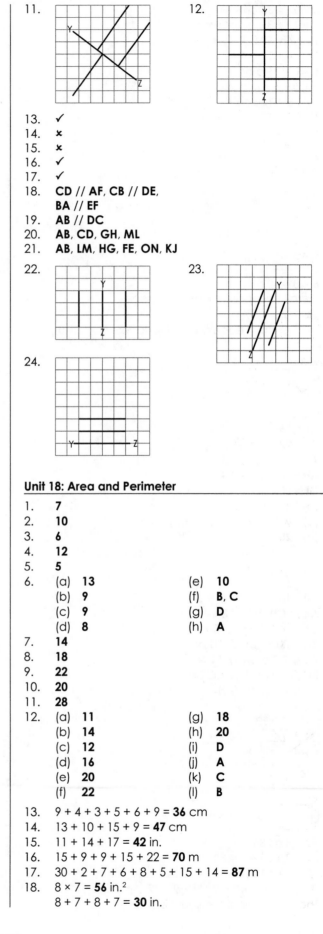

11.
12.
13. ✓
14. ✗
15. ✗
16. ✓
17. ✓
18. **CD // AF, CB // DE,**
    **BA // EF**
19. **AB // DC**
20. **AB, CD, GH, ML**
21. **AB, LM, HG, FE, ON, KJ**
22.
23.
24.

## Unit 18: Area and Perimeter

1. **7**
2. **10**
3. **6**
4. **12**
5. **5**
6. (a) **13**   (e) **10**
   (b) **9**    (f) **B, C**
   (c) **9**    (g) **D**
   (d) **8**    (h) **A**
7. **14**
8. **18**
9. **22**
10. **20**
11. **28**
12. (a) **11**   (g) **18**
    (b) **14**   (h) **20**
    (c) **12**   (i) **D**
    (d) **16**   (j) **A**
    (e) **20**   (k) **C**
    (f) **22**   (l) **B**
13. 9 + 4 + 3 + 5 + 6 + 9 = **36** cm
14. 13 + 10 + 15 + 9 = **47** cm
15. 11 + 14 + 17 = **42** in.
16. 15 + 9 + 9 + 15 + 22 = **70** m
17. 30 + 2 + 7 + 6 + 8 + 5 + 15 + 14 = **87** m
18. 8 × 7 = **56** in.²
    8 + 7 + 8 + 7 = **30** in.

19. $3 \times 12 = $ **36** cm²
    $3 + 12 + 3 + 12 = $ **30** cm
20. $13 \times 4 = $ **52** ft.²
    $13 + 4 + 13 + 4 = $ **34** ft.
21. $6 \times 6 = $ **36** cm²
    $6 + 6 + 6 + 6 = $ **24** cm
22. $15 \times 8 = $ **120** cm²
    $15 + 8 + 15 + 8 = $ **46** cm
23.

8 cm
4 cm | | 4 cm
8 cm

$4 + 8 + 4 + 8 = $ **24** cm
Andrew needs **24 cm** of wire.

24.

8 cm
6 cm

$6 \times 8 = $ 48 m²
Mercy sweeps **48 m²** of floor space.

25. $240 \div 4 = $ 60 yd.
    The length of each side of the square field is **60 yd.**

## Review 3

1.

2. (a) **16**
   (b) **22**
3. **9, 2**
4. **AH > HG, GF > HG,**
   **GF > FE**
5. (a) **z**          (c) **y**
   (b) **y**          (d) **z, x, w, y**
6. (a) **20**         (f) **16**
   (b) **10**         (g) **18**
   (c) **14**         (h) **24**
   (d) **11**         (i) **B**
   (e) **18**         (j) **D**
7. **AB // CD, HG // ML**
8. $24 + 14 + 6 + 9 + 18 + 5 = $ **76 in.**
9. **BA // KL** or **DC // HJ** or
   **AL // BC** or **AL // JK** or
   **BC // ED** or **JK // HG** or
   **AL // ED** or **AL // HG**
10.

11.

12. $32 \times 8 = $ **256** in.²
    $32 + 8 + 32 + 8 = $ **80** in.
13. $12 \times 12 = $ **144 cm²**
14. $9 + 9 + 9 + 9 + 9 + 9 + 9 + 9 = 72$ cm
    The perimeter of the figure is **72 cm.**

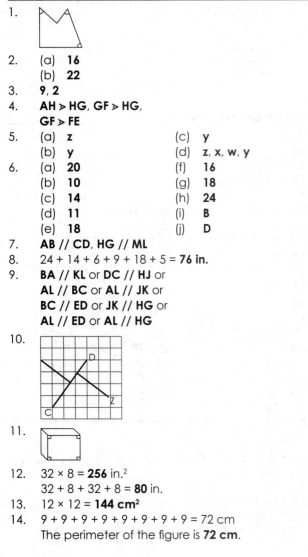

15. $15 \times 2 = 30$ in.
    Its length is 30 in.
    $15 + 30 + 15 + 30 = 90$ in.
    The perimeter of the box is **90 cm.**
16. $20 \times 8 = 160$ in.²
    The area of the room is **160 m².**
17. $30 \times 15 = 450$ in.²
    $450 - 80 = 370$ in.²
    The area of the remaining wrapping paper was
    **370 in.²**
18. $14 \times 11 = 154$ cm²
    $154 \times 2 = 308$ cm²
    The area of the piece of drawing paper was
    **308 cm².**
19. $25 - 13 = 12$ cm
    $13 + 9 + 12 + 7 + 25 + 16 = 82$ cm
    The perimeter of the remaining cardboard is **82 cm.**
20. $5 + 8 + 5 + 8 + 5 + 8 + 5 + 8 = 52$ cm
    The perimeter of the two stickers is **52 cm.**

## Final Review

1. (a) **AB > GH, CD > GH**
   (b) **AB//CD**
2. **5:30 P.M.**

   15 min.          30 min.
   |—————|————————————|
   4:45 P.M.    5:00 P.M.          5:30 P.M.

3. (a) $300$ cm $+ 7$ cm $= $ **3 m 7 cm**
   (b) $43,000$ g $+ 210$ g $= $ **43,210 g**
   (c) $80,000$ mL $+ 10$ mL $= $ **80,010 mL**
   (d) $4,000$ m $+ 40$ m $= $ **4,040 m**
4. (a) **books**
   (b) **40**
   (c) $55 - 15 = $ **40**
   (d) $20 - 5 = $ **15**
   (e) $15 + 5 = $ **20**
5. (a) **$3.30**
      $2.35 + $0.95 = $3.30
   (b) **$1.40**
      $2.00 + $1.60 = $3.60
      $5.00 - $3.60 = $1.40
   (c) **$0.30 / 30¢**
      $0.95 + $1.35 = $2.30
      $2.30 - $2 = $0.30
   (d) **notebook, pen, and sharpener**
      $1.60 + $1.35 + $0.95 = $3.90
6. (a) $\dfrac{3 \times 3}{7 \times 3} = \dfrac{9}{\mathbf{21}}$
   (b) $\dfrac{2 \times 4}{4 \times 4} = \dfrac{\mathbf{8}}{16}$
   (c) $\dfrac{8 \times 4}{11 \times 4} = \dfrac{32}{\mathbf{44}}$
   (d) $\dfrac{4 \times 3}{9 \times 3} = \dfrac{\mathbf{12}}{27}$
7. (a) $\dfrac{8 \div 4}{12 \div 4} = \dfrac{\mathbf{2}}{\mathbf{3}}$
   (b) $\dfrac{3 \div 3}{6 \div 3} = \dfrac{\mathbf{1}}{\mathbf{2}}$
   (c) $\dfrac{6 \div 2}{8 \div 2} = \dfrac{\mathbf{3}}{\mathbf{4}}$

Singapore Math Practice Level 3B

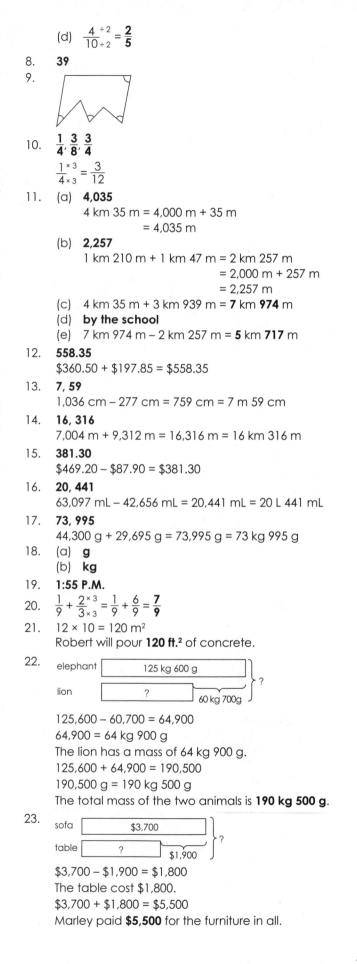

(d) $\frac{4 \div 2}{10 \div 2} = \frac{2}{5}$

8. **39**

9.

10. $\frac{1}{4}, \frac{3}{8}, \frac{3}{4}$

$\frac{1 \times 3}{4 \times 3} = \frac{3}{12}$

11. (a) **4,035**
    4 km 35 m = 4,000 m + 35 m
    $\qquad$ = 4,035 m
    (b) **2,257**
    1 km 210 m + 1 km 47 m = 2 km 257 m
    $\qquad$ = 2,000 m + 257 m
    $\qquad$ = 2,257 m
    (c) 4 km 35 m + 3 km 939 m = **7** km **974** m
    (d) **by the school**
    (e) 7 km 974 m − 2 km 257 m = **5** km **717** m

12. **558.35**
    $360.50 + $197.85 = $558.35

13. **7, 59**
    1,036 cm − 277 cm = 759 cm = 7 m 59 cm

14. **16, 316**
    7,004 m + 9,312 m = 16,316 m = 16 km 316 m

15. **381.30**
    $469.20 − $87.90 = $381.30

16. **20, 441**
    63,097 mL − 42,656 mL = 20,441 mL = 20 L 441 mL

17. **73, 995**
    44,300 g + 29,695 g = 73,995 g = 73 kg 995 g

18. (a) **g**
    (b) **kg**

19. **1:55 P.M.**

20. $\frac{1}{9} + \frac{2 \times 3}{3 \times 3} = \frac{1}{9} + \frac{6}{9} = \frac{7}{9}$

21. 12 × 10 = 120 m²
    Robert will pour **120 ft.²** of concrete.

22. 

    elephant | 125 kg 600 g
    lion | ? | 60 kg 700g

    125,600 − 60,700 = 64,900
    64,900 = 64 kg 900 g
    The lion has a mass of 64 kg 900 g.
    125,600 + 64,900 = 190,500
    190,500 g = 190 kg 500 g
    The total mass of the two animals is **190 kg 500 g**.

23. 

    sofa | $3,700
    table | ? | $1,900

    $3,700 − $1,900 = $1,800
    The table cost $1,800.
    $3,700 + $1,800 = $5,500
    Marley paid **$5,500** for the furniture in all.

24. 

    | 93 km 650 m | 6 km 770 m |
    Town A $\qquad$ Town B $\qquad$ Town C

    93,650 + 6,770 = 100,420
    100,420 m = 100 km 420 m
    The ship travels **100 km 420 m** altogether.

25. 

    Saturday | 10 L 50 mL
    Sunday | 8 L 960 mL

    10,050 + 8,960 = 19,010
    19,010 mL = 19 L 10 mL
    Mary cooked 19 L 10 mL of chicken soup on Sunday.
    10,050 + 19,010 = 29,060
    29,060 mL = 29 L 60 mL
    The total volume of chicken soup that she cooked on
    both days was **29 L 60 mL**.

### Challenge Questions

1. Use 'Guess and Check' method.
   (2 × $10) + (1 × $5) + (4 × $1) + (2 × 25¢) + (2 × 10¢)
   = $29.70
   The bills and coins she gave the cashier were **two
   ten-dollar bills**, **one five-dollar bill**, **four one-dollar bills**,
   **two quarters**, and **two dimes**.

2. 
   | 1 km | 1 km |
   Jamie's house $\qquad$ garden $\qquad$ school

   2 × 1 = 2 km
   The distance from Jamie's house to her school is
   **2 km**.

3. Use 'Guess and Check' method.
   12 + 34 = 46
   43 + 21 = 64
   A = **1**, B = **2**, C = **3**, D = **4**

4. 1 m + 50 cm = 1 m 50 cm
   Plant B is 1 m 50 cm tall.
   1 m − 5 cm = 100 cm − 5 cm = 95 cm
   Plant C is 95 cm tall.
   Plant B is the tallest and Plant C is the shortest.
   1 m 50 cm + 95 cm = 2 m 45 cm
   The total height of the tallest and the shortest plants is
   **2 m 45 cm**.

5. 

   Tokyo: 7 A.M.
   Singapore: 6 P.M.

   The time of his flight in Singapore was **11 P.M.** on
   **September 13**.

6. $\frac{1 \times 2}{4 \times 2} = \frac{2}{8}$

   $\frac{2}{8}$ of the string was immersed in oil and water.

$\frac{1}{8} \to 5$ cm

$\frac{2}{8} \to 5 \times 2 = 10$ cm

$\frac{8}{8} \to 5 \times 8 = 40$ cm

The total length of the string was **40 cm**.

7.  first bill
    second bill
    third bill

    $45

    9 units → $45
    1 unit → $45 ÷ 9 = $5
    13 units → $5 × 13 = $65
    Ken has **$65**.

8.  | 12 hours earlier |

    12:00 P.M.             12:00 A.M.
    Christmas Eve          Christmas Day
    (New York)             (Singapore)

    The time in New York will be **12:00 P.M.** on **Christmas Eve**.

9.  | 1 whole |

    Father        Simon  Mother Brother

    $8 \times 2 = 16$
    There were **16** pieces of pizza at first.

10. There are 4 bills. One is 5 times the amount of the other.

    $5

    $1

    $5 \times \$1 = \$5$
    $\$5 + \$1 = \$6$
    $\$1 \times \$6 = \$6$
    The change was $6.
    $\$25 - \$6 = \$19$
    The groceries were **$19**.

11. $30 \div 3 = 10$
    $10 \times 1$ in. = 10 in.
    The bean plant will grow **10 in.** after 30 days.

12. From the given numbers,
    $118 + 159 = 277$
    $387 + 513 = 900$
    $118 + 269 = 387$
    $277 + 623 = 900$
    $623 - 269 = 354$   or   $513 - 159 = 354$
    The missing number is **354**.